Theory of Nothing

Russell K. Standish

To order additional copies, please contact us.
BookSurge, LLC
http://www.booksurge.com
+1 866 308 6235
orders@booksurge.com

Contents

1 Schrödinger's Cat   **1**

2 Beginnings   **21**
   2.1 Emergence   22
   2.2 The Observer   28
   2.3 Complexity, entropy and all that   31
   2.4 Computing Complexity   39

3 Theory of Nothing   **41**
   3.1 More than can be seen   41
   3.2 Ensembles   43
   3.3 Spontaneous Symmetry Breaking   55

4 A Theory of Observation   **57**
   4.1 Occam's Razor   57
   4.2 The White Rabbit Problem   59
   4.3 Time   63
   4.4 Observer Moments   66
   4.5 Measure   67
   4.6 Functionalism   69
   4.7 Computationalism   71

5 Anthropic Reasoning   **81**
   5.1 Anthropic Principle   81

5.2   Doomsday Argument   84
5.3   Anthropic Selection   89
5.4   Ants are not conscious   90
5.5   Mirror Tests   94

6   Evolution   97
6.1   Evolution in the Multiverse   101
6.2   Creativity   102
6.3   Creating the creative machine   106
6.4   Simplest Complexity Generator   113

7   Quantum Mechanics   115
7.1   Deriving the Postulates   118
7.2   Correspondence Principle   120
7.3   Extreme Physical Information   123
7.4   Marchal's theory of COMP   125
7.5   Comparing the three "roads" to Quantum
      Mechanics   130
7.6   Ensemble theory   131

8   Immortality   137
8.1   Arguments against QTI   138
      8.1.1   Maximum possible age   138
      8.1.2   Dementia   143
      8.1.3   Single tracks through Multiverse ar-
              gument   144
      8.1.4   Doomsday argument   145
8.2   ASSA vs RSSA   146
8.3   Applications   147
8.4   Decision Theory   150
8.5   More Scenarios   152

9   Consciousness and Free Will   155
9.1   Illusions   155
9.2   Time   161

9.3 Self Awareness 163
9.4 Free Will 166
9.5 Why self-awareness and free will? 169
9.6 Responsibility 173
9.7 Interpretations of QM 175
9.8 Realism 176
9.9 Other 'isms in Philosophy of the Mind . . 176

10 Summing up   181

A Basic mathematical ideas   187
   A.1 Exponents, logarithms, and functions . . . 188
   A.2 Complex numbers 189
   A.3 Vector Spaces 194
        A.3.1 Hermitian and Unitary operators . 197
        A.3.2 Eigenvalues and Eigenvectors . . . 198
   A.4 Sets 199
        A.4.1 Infinite Cardinality 200
        A.4.2 Measure 203
   A.5 Sum and Difference — Calculus 203

B How Soon until Doom?   207

C Anthropic selection   213

D Derivation of QM   217

List of Figures

2.1   Pareto front   29
2.2   Complexity can be computed by counting
      the number of equivalent descriptions . .   33
2.3   Jorge Luis Borges's fantastic Library of Ba-
      bel   34
2.4   Boltzmann-Gibbs formula   36
2.5   Ideal Gas Law   38

4.1   Constructing the Cantor set   66

5.1   Two possible scenarios for population sizes
      into the future   86
5.2   World population from 500 BCE to present   88
5.3   Distribution of national populations in the
      year 2000   91

9.1   Müller-Lyer illusion   158

A.1 $\sqrt{2}$ is an irrational number   190
A.2   Polar coordinates   191
A.3   Addition of two vectors   195
A.4   The inner product   195
A.5   Eigenvectors of a linear map   198
A.6   Cantor's diagonalisation argument   202

A.7   An integral is the area under a curve be-
      tween two limits   204
A.8   A derivative is the slope of a curve at a point 205

B.1   Plot of expected time to doom from 1000BCE
      to present   212

List of Tables

7.1   Marchal's menagerie of modal logics . . .   129

B.1   Historical World Population 209

B.2   Results for population growth r, α and expected time to doomsday ($\langle \tau \rangle$) for population data. 211

Chapter 1

A Brush with Schrödinger's Cat

Schrödinger's cat's a mystery cat,
he illustrates the laws;
The complicated things he does
have no apparent cause;
He baffles the determinist,
and drives him to despair
For when they try to pin him down
— the quantum cat's not there!

Schrödinger's cat's a mystery cat,
he's given to random decisions;
His mass is slightly altered
by a cloud of virtual kittens;
The vacuum fluctuations print
his traces in the air
But if you try to find him,
the quantum cat's not there!

Schrödinger's cat's a mystery cat,
he's very small and light,

And if you try to pen him in,
he tunnels out of sight;
So when the cruel scientist
confined him in a box
With poison-capsules,
triggered by bizarre atomic clocks,
He wasn't alive, he wasn't dead,
or half of each; I swear
That when they fixed his eigenstate
— he simply wasn't there!

Anonymous, with apologies to *T.S. Eliot*

One night in 1995, cycling home from work in the dark, a car speeds through the intersection in front of me, without a glance in my direction. I brake, narrowly missing the car. What, I wonder, might have happened if I'd been cycling a little faster, or the car came through the intersection two seconds later.

Instead of thanking the gods for this escape, my mind turned to the fate of that well known mythical beast, Schrödinger's cat. For the uninitiated, Schrödinger's cat is an ill-fated moggie placed in a sealed box with a radioactive atom and a cannister of poison gas. The atom has a 50% chance of decaying in an hour. If the atom decays, it triggers the release of the poison, killing the cat instantly. After one hour, the scientist opens the box. There is 50-50 chance that the cat is still alive.

What has this to do with speeding cars on a dark night? Bear with me, as it shall become clear after a brief detour through the foundations of quantum mechanics, our most fundamental theory of matter.

What is the state of the cat just prior to the box being opened? Common sense tells us that the cat should be either alive or dead, with equal probability. However,

3

this is not what quantum mechanics tells us. Quantum mechanics describes the decaying atom as a mixed state of being both decayed and whole simultaneously. Only when it is observed, does the state become definitely one or the other. Does this mean that quantum mechanics is merely describing our ignorance of the state of affairs — that the atom is really one or the other all the time? Einstein thought so, and in a famous paper published a thought experiment with his colleagues Podolsky and Rosen to test this[45]. Unfortunately for Einstein, it turns out that nature really does behave the way quantum mechanics says it does — when the Einstein-Podolsky-Rosen thought experiment was finally done for real, it was found that things like that radioactive atom really are in a mixed state prior to being observed[6].

Just as the atom is in a mixed state, then so must be the cat in Schrödinger's thought experiment, as the states are perfectly correlated. There lies the paradox. This puzzling conundrum has absorbed some of the brightest minds of 20th century physics and philosophy. Schrödinger's paper in which he introduces his cat[114] is considered one of the more important foundational papers in the field of *interpretations of quantum mechanics.*

Quantum mechanics as a mathematical theory works extremely well without an interpretation. Physicists can compute the outcomes of experiments precisely, as these usually involve millions of particles, so probabilities simply become fractions of the total number of particles, which can be accurately measured. This way of using quantum mechanics is known as the "shut up and calculate" approach. However, scenarios like Schrödinger's cat, or the Einstein-Podolsky-Rosen example demonstrate that our commonsense, or "folk" understanding of reality is wrong, and so the question of what it all means

demands an interpretation of quantum mechanics. A
number of interpretations have been proposed, but I will
mention only the two most popular — the *Copenhagen
Interpretation*, in which the system's state collapses to
yield a definite value (a so-called *eigenvalue*) for any observed quantity, and the *Many Worlds Interpretation*[39],
(MWI) in which all possible eigenvalues exist as independent parallel universes after measurement, with no change
to the overall state.

This book is not the place to debate the merits of one
interpretation of quantum mechanics over another — numerous authors have done a far better job of this than I
can do, for example David Deutsch mounts a persuasive
argument in favour of the Many Worlds Interpretation in
the first chapter of *Fabric of Reality*[43]. I have long been
a convert to the many worlds point of view, for as long as
I have realised that an interpretation is necessary. Competing interpretations all have conceptual difficulties — if
the quantum state has some ontological reality (ie physically "exists" in some sense) then the collapse happens
faster than the speed of light conflicting with special relativity's notion of locality. State collapse also appears to
be something ad hoc, a nonunitary process grafted onto
the normal unitary evolution described by Schrödinger's
equation (these terms will be explained in chapter 7). The
Many Worlds Interpretation by contrast does not postulate this nonunitary collapse — instead a nonunitary process appears in the view "from the inside", or first person
viewpoint of the observer. There is no conflict with special relativity, since any "collapse" takes place within the
mind of the observer, a necessarily localised event.

Even if you are not a many worlder, or would prefer to sit on the fence, it is well worth the while taking the many worlds idea seriously to see what conse-

quences there might be for our understanding of reality. In this book, we will go much further than just the MWI of quantum mechanics. We shall consider the possibility that the reality we inhabit is but one of all possible *descriptions*. It might seem strange to think of reality being a description, a confusion between "the map and the territory" as it were. Yet maps are maps precisely because they leave out details of the territory to make the overall relationships between landmarks clear. Our descriptions, on the other hand record everything that is possible to know about the "territory" — in fact we will identify these descriptions with the quantum mechanical state function later on. Our descriptions are so detailed that perhaps it no longer makes sense to ask Stephen Hawking's question "what breathes fire into them?"[59]. Putting Hawking's question aside, a question that has no answer in conventional ontologies, we note that the collection of all possible descriptions has zero complexity, or information content. This is a consequence of algorithmic information theory, the fundamental theory of computer science. There is a mathematical equivalence between the Everything, as represented by this collection of all possible descriptions and Nothing, a state of no information. That some of the descriptions must describe conscious observers who obviously observe something, gives us a mechanism for getting Something from Nothing: *Something* is the "inside view" of *Nothing*. Hence my book's title *Theory of Nothing*.

Returning to our unfortunate incarcerated moggie, I wondered what the cat experiences *from the cat's own point of view*, instead of the customary scientist's point of view in the Schrödinger cat experiment. Clearly, the cat can never experience death. The Many Worlds Interpretation assures us that alternative worlds in which the

cat survives really do exist. The only possible experience
for the cat is after spending a fretful hour with nothing
happening, the lid of the box is opened by the scientist, and the cat survives. Stepping into the Schrödinger
death chamber becomes an experimental test of the Many
Worlds Interpretation. It is a peculiar sort of test as you
can only convince yourself of the truth of the MWI —
any outsider looking on will observe you dying with the
usual probabilities. In short, there is a disparity between
the *first person viewpoint* of the cat, and what we will
call later the *first person plural viewpoint* that any two
scientists, practising objectivity, would agree upon.

Reflecting on my incident with the car, I realised that
each and every one of us plays quantum roulette. Every
day, we are all cats in Schrödinger's morbid experiment.
The instrument of death varies in each case, the probability values vary, it may be the speeding car, it may be the
bolt of lightning out of the blue. However, every second
of the day, there is some non-zero probability that we may
die. Conversely, there is always some probability that we
survive. The many worlds interpretation of quantum mechanics tells us we experience survival. I had discovered
the *Quantum Theory of Immortality*. It turned out I was
not the only one thinking along these lines, nor was I
the first. I had discovered quantum physics' "dirty little
secret". I've met many people who have independently
come across this notion, including a number of well re-
spected physicists. Only now it is becoming acceptable
to talk about it — it is an idea whose time has come.

In 1997, New Scientist published an article describing
a thought experiment attributed to Max Tegmark[28]. In
it, the experimenter stands in front of a quantum machine gun, which is controlled by a stream of particles
whose "quantum spin" can point either up or down, each

with a 50 per cent probability. If the spin is measured to be up, the gun fires a bullet; if it is down, it doesn't. The particle exists in a superposition of the two states, and according to the Copenhagen interpretation, when the measurement is made, the particle chooses either up (bullet) or down (no bullet). In Tegmark's thought experiment, the experimenter should experience immortality if the many worlds interpretation is true.

Also around this time, David Deutsch published *The Fabric of Reality*[43], in which he argues that the long sought-after fundamental theory of science, the so called *Theory of Everything* will turn out to be an amalgam of four quite distinct areas of thought: the many worlds interpretation; the theory of computation, also known as *algorithmic information theory; Darwinian theory of evolution*; and *Popperian falsification*. Whilst I did not start out with the aim of developing Deutsch's ideas, it proved remarkable that the theories which I will talk about in this book are a blend of Deutsch's first three strands.

Max Tegmark released a colossal position paper on the Internet in 1996, in which he argued that perhaps the "Theory of Everything" is merely an ensemble theory — a theory of parallel realities constructed from the logical possibilities available in mathematics. This paper was picked up by New Scientist in 1998, when I first became aware of it. It struck me as a new way of short-circuiting the Kuhnian paradigm block — publish your crazy stuff on the Internet, let people pull the ideas apart and get the arguments going. In the longer term, this can lead to publishable scientific theory. Tegmark's paper was accepted for publication in a peer-reviewed journal in 1998[134].

More influential to my thinking than the ideas in Tegmark's paper however, was the creation of an email discussion group in 1998, called the *Everything list*[1]. This list attracted some of the brightest, and unconventional thinkers in the world, and linked them via the Internet. Unlike many other Internet discussion fora, which often seem to be dominated by people who like the sound of their own ideas, the quality of discussion on this list remains particularly high. There is a lot of highly stimulating material in these archives, mixed up with wild speculations the authors have since thought the better of. Indeed, some 12 of my scientific publications trace back, in varying degrees, to topics discussed on the Everything list. Some of these are cited in this book's bibliography. In many ways, this book aims to pull the most important ideas from this list's archive, citing the original messages to allow scholars a way into the archive. This book also attempts a synthesis of the ideas discussed freely on the everything list along with many other ideas, mainstream and subversive from millennia of intellectual thought.

My own "crazy" paper in which I derive the postulates of quantum mechanics from considering a collection of all possible descriptions first appeared on the Internet in 2000. With the help of numerous comments from other scientifically minded people, and from the anonymous referees of the paper, it was accepted for publication in 2004[128]. That paper, for which the conservative conclusion is that quantum mechanics is merely the theory of observation, has a rather more radical message. Perhaps all of the fundamental laws of physics can ultimately be related to some property or other of an observer. Not only is our psyche emergent from the electrical and chemical goings on in our brain, but the laws governing that

---

[1]The archives of the Everything list can be found at
http://groups.google.com/group/everything-list, or alternatively
http://www.mail-archive.com/everything-list@eskimo.com.

chemico-electrical behaviour in turn depend on our psyche. Doing physics is one way to study cognitive science. Studying cognitive science and comparing the results with physics is a test of this hypothesis. Many physicists are sceptical of the many worlds idea, and also of the *anthropic principle* (consistency of observed reality with the observer) as having anything useful to say scientifically. Yet they tie together fundamental physics and cognitive science in such a way as to make this "theory of nothing" scientific in the Popperian sense (falsifiable) in the quite foreseeable event of cognitive science developing its own body of results. The topics I address in this book support this thesis.

Polymaths, or individuals with a detailed knowledge of all branches of science, and of philosophy, are rumoured to have been extinct for centuries. To properly advance the ideas in this book, indeed any putative theory of *everything* requires a polymath — yet I make no claims of being one! I have also taken the liberty of the book format to advance some speculative reasoning that might never see the light of day in a scientific article. Undoubtedly I have made mistakes of reasoning. What is important is that I present my reasoning in as plain a fashion as possible so that you, dear reader can decide for yourself what substance there is to the extraordinary claims contained herein. Unfortunately, this does not make for an easy read. Stephen Hawking famously remarked that each mathematical equation included in a book would halve its sales. Yet my book would be ill-served by eschewing mathematics altogether. Mathematics is a language for describing formal and abstract systems, without which it is very hard to reason about reality at all. I have deliberately constructed this book to only make use of mathematical concepts typically taught at high school to allow people as diverse as physicists, biologists and philosophers to follow the reasoning. I also hope that the material is accessible to the amateur scientist or philosopher, and I provide appendices of mathematical concepts and notation to help those whose mathematical skills are rusty.

It should be mentioned, in passing, that the term "theory of everything" was originally a humorous tagline for efforts by physicists to unify our theories of gravitation with the so called *standard model*, which successfully describes all "fundamental particles": quarks, electrons, protons, neutrinos and so on, along with their interactions via the strong, weak and electromagnetic forces. Of all fundamental physical phenomena, only gravity is left out of the picture. Our best theory of gravitation, Einstein's general theory of relativity works extremely well on the large scale of planets, stars, galaxies and the universe, yet begins to break down on the scale of fundamental particles. General relativity appears to be mathematically incompatible with quantum mechanics, the theory within which the standard model exists. The current best bet for a theory of quantum gravity is string theory, which has been under development since 1970. The theory is computationally difficult to extract predictions from (as is the standard model in fact), needs immensely powerful and technologically unfeasible particle accelerators to test and most bizarrely of all requires that space be at least ten dimensional, a difficulty usually circumvented by assuming that the extra dimensions are folded up so tightly as to not be noticeable.

Alternatives to string theory are also being developed, such as loop quantum gravity. Lee Smolin has written an excellent introductory book on these attempts called "Three Roads to Quantum Gravity"[122]. I believe physicists will ultimately be successful in their endeavours, even if the answer turns to be different from any current physical theory, if only because unified theories are algorithmically simpler in the sense of Occam's razor, a topic I will discuss in §4.1. However, this book is not about quantum gravity "theories of everything". Quantum gravity will never explain the properties of polypeptide chemistry, let alone the behaviour of a human being. Thus the claim of being a theory of everything is overly grandiose, and the label "theory of everything" should be treated with the levity with which it was originally proposed. Instead, this book is about *ensemble* "theories of everything", of the sort that David Deutsch and Max Tegmark have proposed. I will argue that these sorts of theories have implications in all sorts of scientific fields, not just physics, so do have a better claim on the title "theory of everything". One should also bear in mind that the more general a theory is, the fewer specific predictions it can make without ad-hoc "boundary assumptions". Thus the ultimate theory of everything is really a theory of nothing at all — a second reading of my book's title.

Thus, a chance meeting with a car one dark evening, a new technology allowing free flowing discussion between creative minds scattered all over the globe and a few well timed books launched me on a breathtaking scientific and spiritual journey. This book is an attempt to share this fascinating journey with the rest of you.

Such a journey may be likened to exploring a mountain range. A helicopter ride over the mountains will leave you with an impression of the mountains' beauty, however you cannot appreciate the scale of the rocks and chasms, nor the chill of the biting wind. This chapter is the helicopter ride, the broad overview of the topic that

doesn't require you to leave your armchair. Even if all
you read of this book is this chapter, you will have learnt
something of a revolutionary understanding of how things
are. Starting with the next chapter, we will head cross-
country to visit the base camps of our mountain range.
You will need some mathematical and scientific tools for
this journey, but I have deliberately avoided technical detail, choosing instead to concentrate on the conceptual
building blocks. I have summarised essential mathematical concepts in appendix A, and other concepts from
physics, computer science, biology and cognitive science
where they first appear in the text. If you find these too
brief for your taste, there are always the internet sources
Wikipedia[2] and the Stanford Encyclopedia of Philosophy[3] to help.

I will now present a map (though not the territory!) of
what you might expect in the rest of the book. In chapter
2 we limber up with some notions from information and
complexity theory, a body of theory that has developed
over the latter half of the 20th century. Many of these
notions, such as *complexity*, and *emergence* are still new
enough that there is no widespread agreement on their
meaning. I use the terms complexity and information in-
terchangeably, the measure of all things being the number
of bytes needed to describe something perfectly. Information is an observer dependent thing. Shakespeare's
"Romeo and Juliet" is nothing more than random gibberish to someone who doesn't know English. The role
of an observer is to attach meanings to descriptions, generating information from data. Emergence is the process
by which new things emerge from combinations of other
things — the wetness of water from the myriads of inter-

---

[2]http://www.wikipedia.org
[3]http://plato.stanford.edu

actions between water molecules, or the mind of person from the electrical impulses coursing through neurons in a brain. Emergence is crucially observer dependent, meaning must be taken into account in order to have emergence.

In chapter 3, we look at the notion of an *ensemble theory of everything*. We have already met the Multiverse, or the ensemble of all possible worlds described by quantum mechanics. However, other ensembles do exist. The speed of light, and the finite age of the universe, means we can only see a certain distance into space. Yet we have no reason to suppose space stops at that boundary. In an infinite space, the same arrangement of molecules and atoms that make up our planet and everything on it at this moment in time will reappear somewhere else. Yet the butterfly effect (the flap of a butterfly's wing may be sufficient to cause a tornado in another part of the Earth's atmosphere) ensures that the remote region will almost surely follow a different trajectory to our own — this is yet another way for alternative possible outcomes to be be real. Functionalism, the idea that our consciousness depends only upon the material arrangement of our brains and bodies implies not only that there is another "you" out there thinking exactly the same thoughts as you, but also that because the other "you" is indistinguishable, your consciousness is actually simultaneously implemented by both copies. When one copy is killed, and the other lives, your conscious experience must follow the living version. Quantum immortality is thus a consequence of functionalism, even in a classical non-quantum world!

Yet more ensembles are considered. Our best theories of reality are mathematical, an observation captured by Wigner's comment[152] on "The unreasonable effectiveness of mathematics". Perhaps all possible mathematical structures exist, as Tegmark suggests, and we just happen to live in one that permits us as conscious observers to exist. This notion of mathematics having an independent existence goes back to Plato's metaphor of a cave. For Plato, all possible mathematical structures, or *ideal forms* exist, and what we see are but "shadows" of these ideal forms dancing upon the wall of our cave. The reason we don't see the ideal forms is that the very process of observation interferes with their perception.

Finally the ensemble theory that I think has most promise. It can be appreciated by another metaphor, due to Jorge Borges. In Borges's Library of Babel, he imagined a library so vast it contained not only all the books ever published with fewer than 1.3 million letters, but also all possible books with fewer than 1.3 million characters typed by monkeys hitting keys on a typewriter. Finding a book in this library is an impossible task. Selecting a book at random from the shelves is more likely to return utter gibberish than (say) the sonnets of William Shakespeare. Cataloging the library is an impossible task — the only thing distinguishing one book from the next is the book's contents, all 1.3 million letters. The catalogue entry for a given book would be as big as the book itself, defeating the purpose of the catalogue.

One could, of course, catalogue only those books written in English, although this would still be a Herculean task. Such a catalogue would not be of much use to a speaker of French (all published works in French are also in this library), nor the visitor from Betelgeuse V. One also has the problem of deciding which of the myriads of books differing by a single word is the authoritative true copy. For every useful scientific tome in the library, myriads of misleading and false works abound.

Thus we should conclude the opposite of what we first supposed. Far from containing the wisdom of the ages, the library is useless, containing no information of worth. Our libraries are useful, not so much for the books they contain, but for the books they don't contain!

In the last ensemble theory I present, all possible descriptions of things exist, of infinite length, composed of symbols from an alphabet of your choice. The alphabet is not important, since translating text from one alphabet to another is a trivial, albeit laborious task. Conventionally an alphabet containing just the two symbols '0' and '1', the binary alphabet of computers is used in discussions. As with Borges's library, the complete ensemble has precisely zero information. The Everything is in fact a Nothing.

In chapter 4, we return to Wigner's comment of the unreasonable effectiveness of mathematics. Mathematics is a language that encodes ideas, moreover it attempts to encode ideas efficiently. Mathematicians look for patterns and relationships between objects, they try to write down the smallest set of statements (called *axioms*) from which other mathematical statements (the *theorems*) can be derived via a logical process of deduction. By harnessing our notions of information, complexity and meaning, we find that we should expect on the balance of probabilities to inhabit a simple universe, one that is amenable to description by a concise language such as mathematics. So if presented with two theories, one simple and one complex, that equally satisfy all experimental results obtained to date, we should expect that the simple theory is more likely to be correct, and remain consistent with future experimental data. The procedure of selecting the simplest of available theories is called *Occam's razor*, what we have is a proof that Occam's razor is an effective procedure.

To attach a meaning to descriptions, observers need to embedded in a temporal dimension. In order to have a bit of information, one needs to perceive a difference between two states, and a time dimension separating those two states. This state of affairs I call the TIME postulate. Computationalism is a possible model of observerhood; not only that an appropriately programmed computer might be conscious, but that we all, as conscious observers, are equivalent to some computer program as yet unknown.

In chapter 5 we introduce the *Anthropic Principle*. This states that reality must be consistent with our existence as observers within that reality, at first blush an unsurprising state of affairs. Yet this very principle places huge constraints on the sorts of properties the universe can have. Many of the fundamental constants of physics have to be "just so", in order for life as we know it to exist. The universe is incredibly fine-tuned. In the context of our theory of nothing, the anthropic principle starts to look suspect. We can easily imagine being embedded in a virtual reality, one that renders a possible universe with perfect fidelity — yet that universe is incompatible with higher order life forms. This experience must be more likely than one in which the anthropic principle holds. So why do we live in a universe so finely-tuned that the anthropic principle must be true? If we are self-aware, there must be a self to be aware of. If that self is not part of our observed reality, or is in some sense deeply incompatible with it, we can conclude that it exists elsewhere — in a reality outside the virtual reality we inhabit. Thus self-awareness ultimately demands the validation of the anthropic principle. If we weren't self-aware though, there would be no logical requirement for the anthropic principle to hold. The validity of the anthropic principle tells us that self-awareness must somehow be necessary to consciousness.

Anthropic reasoning can lead to some surprising conclusions. The most famous anthropic argument is called the *Doomsday Argument*, which argues that we should expect a calamitous drop in human population levels in the next few centuries. Anthropic reasoning also shows that the majority of non-human animals cannot be conscious, a point I would like to stress, has no bearing whatsoever on our moral responsibility to animal welfare.

In chapter 6 we look at Darwin's theory of evolution, one of the greatest intellectual edifice in human thought. Evolution is a far more general process than simply a description of how animals and plants came into being and how their forms changed over time. In the context of the theory of nothing, evolution is the only game in town when it comes to creative processes. The arts, science, the thoughts in your head are all results of evolutionary processes. Even the universe itself is the result of evolution. This observation has implications for the theory of cognition. Not only must reality have random processes embedded in it, but brains must exploit this randomness in order to be creative. This is in contrast with computers, which are engineered to minimise the effect of noise on the system. Brains appear to exploit the butterfly effect so as to be exquisitely sensitive to system noise. As a consequence, I hold that computationalism is strictly false, although probably a useful approximation.

In chapter 7 I take seriously the suggestion that observed reality is the result of an evolutionary process. This leads to a derivation of the fundamental postulates of quantum mechanics. There are a few different ways into this topic, each with its own set of assumptions, but the conclusion seems clear — the weirdness of quantum mechanics is nothing more than a consequence of the process of observation. The weirdness stems from the folk belief that the world can be separated from the observer. The message of quantum mechanics is that the observer is an integral part of reality, and cannot be ignored. The extension of this philosophical point of view is that all laws of physics will eventually be found to relate back to some essential property of the conscious observer — the central thesis of this book.

Chapter 8 revisits the *quantum theory of immortality*, and the many debates it ignited on the Everything list. It is a popular topic of discussion on the Everything list, and has implications for many areas of thought, from philosophical paradoxes, morality and even religion.

Finally in chapter 9, we turn to cognitive science to see what light the theories in this book shed on the classic conundrums of consciousness and free will. Causality flows both ways. Not only is our psyche the end result of an evolutionary process, but the physical world we live in is anthropically selected by our psyche from the Everything ensemble. Free will is a necessary part of our consciousness, it is the source of our creativity. It is also advantageous in an evolutionary setting, as a means of escaping predation, or of avoiding being taken advantage of by our fellow humans. Free will sets up an evolutionary arms race, in which self-awareness is the solution to allowing us to predict our fellow human beings. Free will, self-awareness and consciousness are inextricably linked.

Chapters 2, 3 and 6 are the "legs" of this book, corresponding roughly to the foundation strands David Deutsch talks about in his book "Fabric of Reality". Chapter 4 draws upon the earlier chapters to present a minimal theory of the observer, and is essential for understanding the final three chapters of the book (chapters 7–9). Someone broadly familiar with the material of this book might be able to start with these latter chapters, referring to earlier one as necessary to clarify concepts and terminology. However, even the earlier chapters present new concepts and arguments, or well known concepts in a more precise, but nontraditional manner, so are worth dipping into.

Chapter 2

Beginnings

> In the beginning was the Word, and the Word
> was with God, and the Word was God.
> *Gospel according to John, 1:1*

In the beginning, there was Nothing, *not even a beginning!* From out of this Nothing, emerged everything we see around us today. This book explores an explanation of how and why this happened, and some of the surprising consequences of that explanation.

In Chapter 1, we flew around the mountain range. Now we head cross-country to the base camps.

In order to scale the mountain peak, you need the right equipment. To *understand* scientific theories, you need the right concepts. I don't want to take you on an armchair cruise of this theory. I would like you to understand it. Therefore, the right place to start is a review of the necessary concepts needed to scale the precipices of foundational theories of reality. Many of the labels for these concepts are not even agreed upon by scientists — indeed terms like *emergence* and *complexity* have caused a lot of ink to be spilt in defence of rival conceptions as to what various words might mean mean. These conceptual difficulties spill over into vaster, muddier realms of philosophical thought, in discussions of *life, consciousness* and *free will.*

The concepts I introduce in this chapter are neither right nor wrong. They are part of a conceptual apparatus, a *lexicon* which I have found very useful in navigating the *theory of Nothing.* Of course the debate as to whether these concepts are the most useful formulation of the terms has yet to happen, however in order to make progress in understanding the topics in this book, I have found it is best to frame the discussion using the terms and concepts introduced here.

2.1   Emergence

Informally, *emergence* is the notion that something is *more* than the sum of the parts from which it constructed. Some examples help illustrate this:

- A molecule of water is not wet. Wetness is an emergent property of large numbers of water molecules.

- The dynamical equations of physics is *reversible.* If you were to stop every molecule then send it with same speed back along its previous path in the opposite direction, the system is indistinguishable (at the microscopic level) from the original one. Yet grains of salt do not spontaneously leap back into the salt sellar after the salt was spilt. Macroscopic *irreversibility* is an emergent property of large numbers of molecules,

- A single neuron is not conscious. *Consciousness*[1] is

---
[1]Here, and elsewhere, I take consciousness as a binary property, syntactically equivalent to existence. Something is either conscious

an emergent property of large numbers of neurons firing within a brain.

Thus it appears that emergence stands in opposition to *reductionism*, a paradigm of understanding something by studying its constituent parts. To someone wedded to the notion of reductionism, emergence can appear rather mysterious and strange.

In this book, we have a rather different take on emergence. A *language* is a lexicon of terms and associated concepts, as well as a syntax the defines how the terms can be connected to each other. Clearly, the spoken and written languages we are familiar with are languages in this sense. So are mathematical equations and computer programs. A scientific model is also a language. A model is a well defined formal object, either abstract as in a mathematical model, a computer program, or a physical toy, like the ball-and-stick models used to represent chemical molecules. In the ball-and-stick case, the terms are the balls and sticks, and the syntax is defined by the fact the balls only have holes in certain places, and sticks used to join the balls together can only be placed in the holes. People who work with mathematical or computer models recognise that the components of these systems plug together in similar ways to ball-and-stick models.

For our system of interest, we suppose there to be two languages, which we call the *syntactic* and the *semantic*. The system is completely specified in the syntactic lan-

---

or it is not. People sometimes use "consciousness" to refer to something like awareness, ie there are levels of consciousness ranging from completely unconscious to barely conscious to fully conscious (or even higher levels according to practitioners of transcendental meditation). Susan Greenfield[57] argues that not only can an individual have different levels of consciousness from time to time, but consciousness forms a continuum throughout the animal kingdom. This latter argument is, I believe, devoid of meaning.

guage. For example, a classical gas or liquid consists of
molecules of different types, which have positions and velocities, and the molecules interact with each other with
well defined forces (eg electric force if they're electrically
charged, or Van der Waals forces if they're not). The
molecules, their states (position and velocity) and their
interactions makes up the syntactic language of the classical fluid.

However, as an observer of such a system, it proves
to be impossible to measure the states of all the particles with any degree of precision. Twenty grams of water
(about four teaspoons) contains a staggering number of
molecules of water, a number known as *Avogadro's number*, approximately 6.022×10^{23}. To give some idea of just
how big this number is, imagine being able to measure
the positions of a thousand molecules per second. It will
still take more 500 times the age of the universe to measure the positions of all molecules in a teaspoon of water.
What is even worse is that these systems exhibit what is
known as *molecular chaos.* Chaos theory[55, 46] has been
popularised a lot in popular culture recently, particularly
the so-called *Butterfly effect*, coined by Edward Lorenz in
the 1960s:

> The flapping of a single butterfly's wing to-
> day produces a tiny change in the state of the
> atmosphere. Over a period of time, what the
> atmosphere actually does diverges from what
> it would have done. So, in a month's time,
> a tornado that would have devastated the In-
> donesian coast doesn't happen. Or maybe one
> that wasn't going to happen, does.[131, p141]

Molecular chaos guarantees that even if one *did* know the
starting positions of all the molecules, the butterfly effect

ensures we cannot track them after a very short period of time.

However, fluids are actually quite predictable and orderly. We can write down mathematical equations describing fluid dynamics. Chaos has not limited our ability to follow the behaviour of the fluid as a whole. However, to do so, we have introduced a second language, one that contains terms describing density, temperature, current flow and so on, with the syntax given by partial differential equations. Nowhere to be seen is any mention of molecules, and their interaction forces. A *reductionist* might say that there is a relationship, or a mapping between the two different models, and indeed one can recover the continuum laws (fluid dynamics) from performing appropriate averages over molecular descriptions. However, one cannot map the continuum terms directly onto the molecular. It makes *no sense* to speak of the density or flow of a single molecule. Therefore the two languages are *incommensurate*. They both can be used to describe the system, both have their own domain of applicability, and are *consistent* with each other, yet do not share a common vocabulary. This second language is closer to what the observer would use to describe the system — I call it the *semantic* language for reasons that will hopefully become obvious in the next section[2]. Nowhere is the incommensurate nature more clear than considering the *second law of thermodynamics*. This states that a quantity called entropy must always increase in a closed system. Consequently if you play backwards a movie of milk being stirred into coffee, you will see configurations,

---

[2]I could have, and have at times, used the terms *microscopic* and *macroscopic* to refer to these languages. This terminology does tend to imply these sorts of scenarios described by statistical physics, rather than more general case of emergence.

and behaviours such as the coffee "unstirring" that you
will never see happen in the real world. Fluid dynamics
is irreversible. Yet the underlying molecular dynamics is
perfectly reversible — the second law not only doesn't
apply at the molecular level, but is actually meaningless.

Whenever we have a situation like this of two languages used to describe a system, where a concept cannot be mapped simply into the concepts of the other language, we say that this concept is *emergent*[125]. What
has been left implicit in this discussion is the notion of
how good the semantic level is at capturing the properties of the system. For the purposes of this book, this
formulation of emergence is sufficient. However, if the semantic model has little predictive or explanatory power
(eg when everything is explained in terms of malevolent
daemons) then any resulting notion of emergence is un-
interesting. It is desirable to have a characterisation of
what constitutes a good semantic description of a system. Recently, McGregor and Fernando formalised this
notion of emergence using information theoretic concepts,
for the particular case of the syntactic system being a *dynamical system*[97]. Interestingly, in saying what emergence is, we have made no mention of multiple, interacting parts, which is typically included in descriptions of
emergence[5].

However, the intractability of computing some macro-
scale behaviour from the microscopic description *is* a
paradigmatic mechanism for emergence. Bedau[12] calls
the notion of emergence presented here *nominal emergence*. Nominal emergence includes concepts which are
"resultant", for example the density of a fluid, which can
be computed from the dividing the number of particles
in a given volume by the size of the volume. He proposes two more stringent versions of emergence, which

he calls *weak* and *strong* emergence. These emergences are characterised by a *computational irreducibility*[153] of the semantic model from the syntactic. This means that the only way of using the syntactic model to predict the behaviour of the system is to simulate it completely. An example from the subject of *n*-body physics is illustrative. A two body system with an inverse square force can be separated into two one-body problems, whose trajectories can be described by a *conic section*[3].

However, as soon as you add one more particle, it turns out to be impossible to reduce the system to a simpler one,[4] except in special circumstances. The behaviour of a 3-body system can only be determined by simulating it computationally.

The difference between weak and strong emergence comes from the notion of downwards causation. If a system behaves according to an emergent law at the semantic level of description, we can say that the constituent components must behave as if this emergent law is influencing the behaviour of the components. This is called *downward causation*. In the case of *weak* emergence, the syntactic behaviour of the systems fully explains the outcome — there is no *actual* downward causation, merely the appearance of it. With *strong* emergence however, the downward causation is real. If the emergent phenomenon wasn't present, the particles would behave otherwise. This form of emergence is often associated with

---

[3]Take a cone, and slice it. The shape of the cut is called a conic section. It may be a circle, ellipse, parabola or hyperbola.

[4]In 1892 Heinrich Bruns proved that not all the integrals involved in a 3-body problem could be expressed in a closed form. In 1913, Karl Sundman found a convergent series approximating the solution to the 3-body problem, but its convergence is too slow to be practical. The only effective means of solving the 3-body problem is numerical integration of the equations of motion.

mental aspects of life that resist reductionist explanations, such as consciousness and free-will.[5]

2.2   The Observer

Science has an uneasy relationship with observers. Science is meant to be *objective*, or observer-independent. Traditionally science handles this by removing the observer from the picture altogether, to the point where the language in scientific papers can be quite stilted and formal. For example, it is often considered unacceptable to write "I added 10mℓ of 18 molar sulfuric acid to the solution" — instead one must write the impersonal "10mℓ of 18 molar sulfuric acid was added to the solution".

The syntactic language mentioned above seems to be objective — it is said to be the language in which the system is completely specified. However, in the real world, the syntactic language often appears to be a semantic language of some deeper level of explanation. A molecular description makes way for an atomic description, which in turn makes way for an subatomic (or electronic) description, and still deeper layers with nuclear description, and quantum chromodynamics (theory of quark interactions). The phenomena on each level emerges out of the deeper level descriptions. There is a strong feeling among physicists that quantum chromodynamics is not the end of this hierarchy, and that quarks might emerge from string theory, or some other theory of quantum gravity[122].

The semantic language on the hand is completely observer dependent. The system itself does not require a description in the semantic level in order to exist. Its purpose is entirely one of convenience for the observer.

---

[5]I shall argue later that *anthropic selection* with the *Multiverse* constitutes a paradigmatic example of strong emergence.

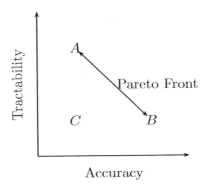

Figure 2.1: Any system description will trade tractability with accuracy. A useful description will not be dominated by any other description in both of these characteristics. In this example, description A is more tractable, and more comprehensible than B, but less accurate. C is less tractable and less accurate than either A or B, and so is said to be Pareto dominated by both A and B. The curve connecting Pareto dominant descriptions is called a *Pareto front*.

It allows the observer to predict the system's behaviour without having to resort to an intractable computation. There is not even one right semantic language. There is usually a tradeoff between tractability and comprehension on one hand, and accuracy on another. The difference between a *model* and a *simulation* might be that a model is for the purpose of understanding the phenomenon of interest, whereas a simulation's purpose is forecasting. Any useful semantic description of a phenomenon will lie on a *Pareto* front (see Fig 2.1) trading tractability with accuracy.

Nevertheless, every semantic language defines a frame

of reference. In the sense that two observers agree upon
a language, they can meaningfully communicate, and the
language is not completely subjective. If two observers
do not agree upon a language, they cannot communicate
at all.

The two big pillars of 20th century science, Relativity and Quantum Mechanics *require* the presence of observers as an integral part of their theories. In relativity,
properties of objects such as mass, length and so on depend on the relative speed of the observer. One can only
eliminate the observer by selecting a particular frame of
reference, often that of the object itself, as though it were
an observer, so one speaks of "rest mass", and so on. In
quantum mechanics, the properties objects have depend
on what the observer chooses to measure. According to
the Heisenberg uncertainty principle, the theoretical minimum experimental error in measuring the position of a
particle is inversely proportional to the experimental error of the particle's position. If you know precisely where
something is, you cannot measure its momentum, and
vice versa. This so strongly contradicts the notion that
science is observer independent, that people have struggled to find an *interpretation* of quantum mechanics in
which the observer disappears. The *Many Worlds Interpretation* is just such an interpretation. By assuming
other worlds where observers measure the *conjugate* properties to the properties measured in this world, for example a parallel world in which I measure position when I
measure momentum in this world, we end up with a an
object, the *Multiverse* in which there are no observers at
all. The observers only exist within the individual worlds
making up the Multiverse.

But hang on a minute! Is this not what *post-modernist*
critiques of science have been saying? That science is a

culturally relative activity, having no claim on absolute truth.

The answer is no. Whilst parts of science are undoubtedly culturally relative, there are observer frameworks that all observers must share, in order to be an observer at all. I will talk about some of these observer properties later, and show how parts of fundamental physics are direct consequences of these properties. Science does have a claim on universality when couched in terms of such a "universal observer".

2.3 Complexity, entropy and all that

The next conceptual tool we need is a measure of *complexity*. There is a huge debate about what complexity might mean. Numerous different complexity measures have been proposed by different scientists, each with its own merits. For example, some people might describe the complexity of an animal by the number of cells in its body, or the number of cell types or the length of its genome. If you're studying the fossil record, you would probably have to make do with the numbers of bones in the skeleton, or the organism's size as this is pretty much the only information that gets fossilised.

However, there is one notion of complexity that is formal, and so is likely to be extendible to cover the full range of applications we might want to use complexity measures for. This notion comes from information theory. Complexity is the amount of *information* needed to describe something. It is important to stress here that *information* is not the same thing as *data*. It is very easy to measure the amount of data you have. For example, a brand new 100GB disk drive contains exactly the same amount of data (100GB worth) as one that has been used

for a few years, and is stuffed full of word processing files,
photos, games etc. However, I'm sure you will agree that
the brand new drive has less *information* on it.

Information is data with *meaning*. There has to be a
somebody, an agent whom we will call an *observer* who
imbues the data with meaning. There may well be more
than one observer, and if they agree on the meanings,
then they will agree on information content, if they differ,
then they will disagree on the amount of information too.

The mapping of data to meanings is not unique —
many different data (descriptions) may be interpreted as
meaning the same thing by the observer. For example,
consider Shakespeare's *Romeo and Juliet*. In Act II,ii, line
58, Juliet says "My ears have yet not drunk a hundred
words". If we change the word "drunk" to "heard", your
average theatre goer will not spot the difference. Perhaps
the only one to notice would be a professional actor who
has played the scene many times. Therefore the different
texts differing by the single word "drunk/heard" in this
scene would be considered equivalent by our hypothetical
theatre goer. There will in fact be a whole *equivalence
class* of texts that would be considered to be *Romeo and
Juliet* by our theatre goer.

The amount of information can be determined from
counting the number of descriptions that map to that
meaning — the fewer descriptions, the more information
that data represents[125].

Randomness has a specific meaning in *algorithmic information theory*. For our present purposes, we will employ a slightly different meaning, one that includes the
AIT meaning, but is somewhat broader: a random description has no observable pattern or regularity. A random string has no meaning whatsoever. It turns out
that rather a lot of descriptions are random in this sense

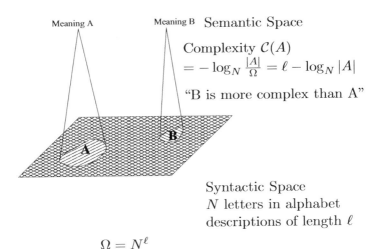

Figure 2.2: Complexity can be computed by counting the number of equivalent descriptions

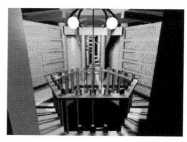

Figure 2.3:   An illustration of Jorge Luis Borges's fantastic   Library   of   Babel   by   Albert   Vass http://www.avass.com (with permission).

— most of them in fact. As a consequence, random data has low complexity. This definition of complexity has the properties of Murray Gell-Mann's *effective complexity*[53].

In the 1940s, Jorge Luis Borges published a short story title "The Library of Babel" (*La biblioteca de Babel* in Spanish), which described a library containing books made up from all combinations of letters. Within this fantastic library consisted the works of all known authors, such as *Romeo & Juliet*, as well as unknown authors, plus books that are complete gibberish. The big problem with this library, is that to find any particular book within it, you must have a copy of the book to act as in index. Consequently the library is in fact useless. Instead of it being a vast repository of information, it contains no information whatsoever.

In the case of considering information or complexity, the problem of observers gets worse. There are many attempts at "brushing the observer under the carpet". For example, in the notion of *physical information*[2], the information content of a system in contact with an environment is given by the difference between the *entropy* of the system and the maximum possible entropy the system could take. This maximal entropy state corresponds to an isolated system at equilibrium, a consequence of the well known *2nd law of thermodynamics* Consequently, physical information is dependent on the environment, and on how far out of equilibrium the system is.

Entropy is usually considered to be an objective property of the system. Denbigh and Denbigh[40] argue this quite forcibly in their book. Given a well-defined set of macroscopic measurements of a system that characterise its state, the entropy of the system in that macroscopic state can be computed by counting the number of microscopic states (positions, momenta and so on of all the particles making up the system), and applying the so called *Boltzmann-Gibbs* formula (see Figure 2.4).

Where does this well-defined set of macroscopic measurements come from? They are the parameters from a model of how the system behaves. For example, the *ideal gas* is one such model, which has 3 parameters: pressure, volume and temperature. The macroscopic state of an ideal gas is given by the triplet of numbers specifying the pressure, volume and temperature. The macroscopic state variables are examples of thermodynamic variables — they are bulk properties of the system, usually an average of a microscopic quantity over all particles making up the system. If the system is assumed to be *ergodic*, i.e. all microstates corresponding to a given total energy are equally likely to be visited by the system, then it can be shown that the Boltzmann-Gibbs entropy defined by thermodynamic state variables is equal to the classical thermodynamics definition of entropy, a definition which any scientist with a handy calorimeter could use to mea-

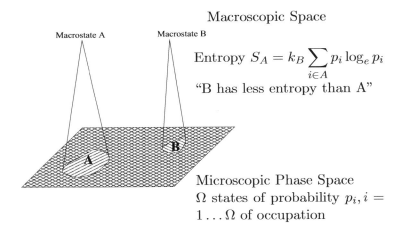

Macroscopic Space

Macrostate A   Macrostate B

Entropy $S_A = k_B \sum_{i \in A} p_i \log_e p_i$

"B has less entropy than A"

Microscopic Phase Space
Ω states of probability $p_i, i = 1 \ldots \Omega$ of occupation

Figure 2.4: Boltzmann-Gibbs formula. Note that if each microscopic state has equal probability $p_i = 1/\Omega$, then $S_A = k_B \log_e \Omega$. Cf figure 2.2, $\mathcal{C}(A) + S_A = S_{\max} = \log \Omega$

sure entropy. This is objective.

However, no model is a replacement for the system itself — real gases do not behave exactly like an ideal gas,
but the behaviour is pretty close. It is possible to have a
system that departs from the thermodynamic description
— by not being spatially uniform for example. One can
create a more complex model with more parameters that
more accurately tracks the behaviour of the system. In
this case the number of microstates corresponding to a
given macrostate is reduced, as the macrostates are more
finely specified, and consequently entropy will be less.
The extreme limit occurs with the viewpoint of a hypothetical being known as Laplace's daemon who is aware
of the positions and motions of all the microscopic particles making up the system. To Laplace's daemon, the
entropy of a system is precisely zero, and remains so for
all time. In this limit, the 2nd law of thermodynamics no
longer applies. Objective entropy is a consequence of the
agreement between scientists to use the thermodynamic
description of matter, and is useful in as far as that model
is a useful model of the phenomena of interest.

Another way of defining complexity is called *Kolmog-
orov-Chaitin-Solomonoff* complexity, after the three
mathematicians who independently invented the measure
around the same time. Computer scientists use a theoretical device called a *Turing machine*. A Turing machine is
an abstract model of a computer, it has a tape on which
it can read and write symbols, and it can move the tape
backwards and forwards. It has an internal state, which
is an integer, and transition table, or set of rules, that
define what the machine does given its state, and the
symbol under its read head. A *universal Turing machine*
is a Turing machine that emulate any other Turing machine by means of an appropriate program introduced via

$$PV = k_B NT$$

P: Pressure

V: Volume

N: Number of molecules

T: Temperature

k_B: Boltzmann's constant

Figure 2.5: Ideal Gas Law

the tape.

The *KCS complexity* of a given string of symbols is given by the length of the shortest program that computes that string when run in a reference universal Turing machine U. What is this reference machine? It turns out not to matter, in a certain sense. Regardless of which universal Turing machine is chosen, the computed complexity will only differ from that of another such machine by a constant, independent of the length of string. KCS complexity turns out to differ by a constant from a version of the complexity computed by counting equivalent descriptions where the role of the observer is taken by U, and the meaning is the output of U.

Nevertheless, the actual numerical value of KCS complexity does depend on the reference machine. Instead of hiding this observer dependence, we really should be embracing it. Any system of scientific interest will have at least one observer observing it — possibly more. These additional observers will have shared terms, concepts and models, otherwise they will not be able to communicate at all. This shared framework of meanings constitutes the reference "observer" that we can use to compute complexity.

2.4 Computing Complexity

The amount of *information* contained in our world is related in a very specific way to the number of descriptions that match our world. Let us pretend for a moment that descriptions are of finite length, L say, and are constructed of a binary alphabet $\{0, 1\}$. Then there are 2^L possible descriptions. Out of all these descriptions, a certain number ω say, correspond to a given meaning. The information content, or complexity of that meaning is given by:

$$C = L - \log_2 \omega = -\log_2 \frac{\omega}{2^L} \qquad (2.1)$$

To see that this equation makes sense, consider a case where the meaning is precisely given by the first ℓ bits — ie all equivalent descriptions start with those ℓ bits (no redundancy), and that all bits after the ℓth position are ignored by the observer. Since all descriptions are L bits long, $\omega = 2^{L-\ell}$, and $C = \ell$.

Equation (2.1) gives a way for defining complexity, even when descriptions are infinite in length. $\frac{\omega}{2^L}$ converges to a finite number between 0 and 1 as $L \to \infty$. This number also satisfies the properties of a probability, which we shall use in our discussion of Occam's Razor (§4.1).

Equation (2.1) also tells us that the complexity of the Everything is zero, just as it is of the Nothing. The simplest set is the set of all possibilities, which is the dual of the empty set.

Chapter 3

Theory of Nothing

> And God said, "Let there be light"; and
> there was light. And God saw that the light
> was good; and God separated the light from
> the darkness. God called the light Day, and
> the darkness he called Night
> *Genesis 1:3–5*

3.1 More than can be seen

In this book we examine a truly preposterous theory, a
theory that all of the reality we see around us, the animals, plants, rocks and seas that make up our planet
Earth; the stars and galaxies that make up the entire visible universe; is but a speck in a truly vaster realm. A
realm of parallel realities, in which you and I exist, but
chance events have different outcomes, and indeed others
in which you and were never born. I do not seek to convince you, dear reader, that this idea is literally true, but
would like to you to open your mind to its possibility, and
to consider the logical consequences of such a proposition.
Along the way, I shall argue that the burden of proof is

actually with the singular view of reality. For there to be a single reality with but a unique strand of history is actually less plausible than for all possible histories to exist side-by-side, and of our only being aware of the one history that we each experience.

Why is the multiple universes theory so preposterous? Part of this is an intellectual tradition whose roots lie with the opening quote of this chapter. A single God creating a single reality, the apex of which is humans, shaped in the likeness of God. Another part is a more pragmatic sense that we can only see what we can see, why suppose any more? This sense has been coded into a principle called *Occam's Razor*, named after William de Ockham: "Entities should not be multiplied unnecessarily". For science, Occam's razor sums up the age of reason. Since many possible explanations for a given datum is possible, Occam's razor gives us a way for choosing the most useful explanation. It is the razor paring off unnecessary complications in the our scientific theories of the world.

To many people, the notion of a plethora of invisible worlds in addition the the world we see about us is an absurd level of complexity, that should be pared away by Occam's razor. Paul Davies, writing an op-ed in the *New York Times*[35] epitomises this point of view. However to assume that more entities means more complexity is a fundamental mistake. Unlike more familiar measures, such as mass, volume or dollar bills, complexity is not additive. Two objects A and B do not necessarily combine to make an object with complexity that is the sum of the two individual objects. Indeed it is possible that the combined entity is *simpler* than either of the two components making it up.

When considering a Multiverse, we could describe the multiverse by writing the histories of all the individual universes side by side. For each fact described in one universe, there will be another universe for which the opposite fact is true. For the Multiverse as a whole, these facts aren't important — we could simply say "everything happens somewhere, sometime". Recall Borges's Library of Babel: the overall complexity is very low, if not zero.

3.2 Ensembles

How can one write a whole book about nothing? Surprisingly, nothing has quite a rich structure. I am also not the only author to be so audacious as to write a book about nothing. For instance, Charles de Bouelles published a book in 1510 called *Liber de Nihilo*, latin for *Book of Nothing*. This book has similar concerns to his — how one can get something from nothing. More recently, John Barrow has also written a *Book of Nothing*[9], which actually deals with the concept of zero, and of the quantum vacuum, neither of which has much bearing on the present topic.

Why a *theory of nothing*? Many people have thought and written about a *theory of everything*, a grand theory from which every fact about the world can be derived, or for the more modest, at least all of physics. Yet such a theory is ultimately futile, the more comprehensive a theory is, the less it seems to contain, and the more has to be inserted in the form of "boundary conditions". Truly, there is no escaping the fact that a theory of everything must ultimately be a theory of nothing.

Richard Feynman[49] wrote that it is very easy to generate a theory containing all the knowledge of physics. Start by writing down all the equations of physics, rearranged so that a zero appears on the right hand side. So we might have equations[1] like:

$$F - ma = 0$$
$$F - \frac{Gm_1m_2}{r_{12}^2} = 0$$
$$\cdots = 0$$

Now the *grand unified theory of physics*, according to Feynman is the deceptively simple equation

$$S = 0$$

where S is defined to be the sum of the left hand sides of all those equations we wrote down before. Clearly, $S = 0$ contains no information whatsoever, all the information is contained in the "definition" of S.

As Max Tegmark pointed out[134], perhaps the ultimate Theory of Everything is an *ensemble theory*. By ensemble, we mean a collection of worlds, all equally real, representing all possibilities[2]. A variety of different ensemble theories have been proposed, before discussing the other competing theories, I would like to introduce my favourite ensemble theory.

Each world consists of an infinite length string of symbols, which can, without loss of generality, be considered as bitstrings. At any point in time, an observer will have observed a finite number of the symbols. Each bitstring

---

[1]If mathematical equations are not your thing, don't worry. The above equations are well known high school physics equations — Feynman's argument doesn't depend on you understanding the equations.

[2]Ensemble is the French word for *set*, a mathematical concept of collections of objects satisfying certain *set axioms*. However, in English, *ensembles* needn't satisfy the set axioms, in particular the axiom of regularity which implies sets cannot contain themselves as members. Often "Everythings" are proposed to contain everything, including themselves.

is as likely as any other, however many strings will be equivalent to others according to an observer, which leads a complexity measure less than the number of bits observed.

The set of all such infinite length descriptions, or the Everything contains no information at all (see §2.4). A subset of the Everything is the set of all descriptions satisfying a set of constraints. The Everything, of course has an empty set of constraints. The set of descriptions matching a set of constraints, and the constraints themselves are what mathematicians call *dual* concepts.

In mathematics, the term *duality* describes a relationship between two categories of objects A and B such that every object of A corresponds to some object of B, and relationships between objects of one category are transformed into equivalent relationships in the other. If one proves a theorem about an object in A, a corresponding theorem about B is also proved by virtue of the duality. This saves a lot of work for the mathematician!

A simple example of a dual concept appears in set theory, and would be familiar to anyone who has studied Venn diagrams at school. The dual of a set could be its complement. In this case, for every element contained in the set A, we can equally say it is not contained in the complement of A, ie ($a \in A \iff a \notin \bar{A}$). Union and intersection operations (see appendix A) are related by duality:

$$x \in A \cup B \iff x \notin \bar{A} \cap \bar{B}$$

The *empty set* is dual to the so called *universal set*.

The Nothing in this picture, refers to the empty set of constraints, so the Nothing is the dual of the Everything. Therefore a *theory of Nothing* is also a *theory of Everything*.[3]

---

[3]I have to acknowledge a certain debt in my ideas to Hal Ruhl,

Sets might seem a slightly strange place to start a discussion on the Everything, as sets come with quite a bit of mathematical baggage called *set axioms*. There are even several different mutually incompatible set axioms to choose from, which make a difference when one talks about infinite sets. However this complication makes no difference to the topic of this book. Whilst much of mathematics is founded on set theory, it is not even the most general mathematical structure. In *Category theory*, sets are simply one category amongst many possible types of category.   There is considerable debate about whether mathematics should be founded on category theory or set theory.

In this book, however, we will use set theory, if for no other reason than that *information theory* is founded upon set theory. Information theory describes how data comes to be imbued with meaning, and as we've seen above allows one to measure the amount of information something has. It is also crucial to the understanding of how *something* arises from *nothing*. Consider how we as observers come to understand anything about the world we live in. Fundamentally, the world we observe, or *phenomena*, is a *description*, a sequence of symbols of some kind coming through our senses. Whether this description corresponds to a *objective reality* of some kind, I shall discuss in a later chapter, however all we can ever know about our world is in the form of this description. Any description can be coded as a binary string, so without loss of generality, information theory is cast in terms of strings of symbols '0' and '1'. The world of our senses is the finite sequence of bits we have observed from our en-

---

who proposed a theory of everything that includes the All and Nothing as duals of each other[110]. Nothing is incomplete, the All is inconsistent.

vironment at any point in time, extracted from an infinite length binary string. Since only a finite number of bits are known at any point in time, our world corresponds to an infinite set of descriptions, each description of infinite length, and each one corresponding to a possible future.

In recent years, *Many Worlds* theories have become quite popular, in which each possible outcome actually occurs in its own parallel universe. The first such theory was originally proposed by Wheeler and de Witt in the 1950s as an interpretation of quantum mechanics. Quantum mechanics has many strange outcomes, such as particles being in two places at once, or having a certain probability of passing through an impenetrable barrier faster than the speed of light. Whilst the mathematical formulation of quantum mechanics is precise, and its predictions well corroborated by experiments, the meaning, or interpretation of quantum mechanics has been debated over the 80 years since quantum theory was developed. In the Many Worlds Interpretation, the one particle in two places scenario is interpreted as the two particles being in different worlds. When you actually measure where the particle is, it will be found in one place. There is also another "you" living in the parallel world that finds the particle in the other place. This collection of worlds is called the *Multiverse*[43].

Quantum Mechanics is not the only way in which the world can be parallel. As we peer out into space, using our most powerful telescopes, we also peer back in time, as light travels at a finite speed c. In the furthest reaches of space that we can see, light has taken almost the entire age of the universe to reach us from the quasars and galaxies that existed at that time. Clearly we cannot see objects so far away that it takes more than the age of the universe for light to travel from them to us.

If we could observe the Big Bang directly, photons from it would appear to be coming from a sphere at the most distant visible distance possible, this sphere is called the *event horizon.*

However, there is no reason to suppose that space stops at the event horizon. Indeed, one popular theory called *inflation* insists that space is very much larger, if not infinite. Beyond the event horizon are other regions of space, some looking very similar to ours, others looking very different. There are only a finite number of quantum states (albeit large) that make up our visible universe, so there is a non-zero probability, that the exact same configuation making up our universe will occur again some where else. If space is infinite, then our universe will certainly appear again, not just once but an infinite number of times. And it will appear an infinite number of more times with slight variations in its history, just as the multitudinous worlds in the Multiverse also appear.

Max Tegmark[136] writing in a volume celebrating John Wheeler's 90th birthday describes a heirarchy of parallel universe theories, the first of which is based on the finite number of quantum states. At level 2, we suppose that inflation occurs at other places of an infinite spacetime continuum. These give rise to a whole plethora of universes, whose fundamental physical constants such as the ratio of electron to proton mass, or the fine structure contant might vary between universes.

Another level 2 parallel worlds scenario arises through considering black holes. By definition, nothing can escape the universe, not even light. By a coincidence, this is also the definition of a black hole, which is a consequence of Einstein's theory of general relativity. Perhaps within black holes in our universes, are complete universes, perhaps with their own conscious observers evolving within them. Perhaps our universe is inside of a black hole itself, part of a bigger universe outside. This notion has been given strength by a recent observation that the physics of five-dimensional black holes is remarkably similar to the physics of our observed universe[115, 149]. Lee Smolin developed an evolutionary theory of universes[121], whereby those universes whose physical parameters allow them to produce more black holes will tend to be more numerous than those producing relatively few black holes. As observers, we are more likely to find ourselves within a universe that produces many black holes, rather than one producing relatively few.

At level 3 of Tegmark's scheme, we have the many world of quantum mechanics, or the Multiverse.[4]

Max Tegmark rekindled interest in parallel universe theory with his paper[134] describing how an ensemble of all consistent mathematical entities might prove to be the "ultimate theory of everything"... 2500 years ago, Plato introduced a theory in which there is a *Plenitude* of *ideal forms*, to which objects in the real world are imperfect copies. Many mathematicians believe that the mathematical objects they study have an independent objective existence, that they are *discovered* through mathematics research, not *created*. This notion is called *Mathematical Platonism*, or *Arithmetical Platonism* by analogy to Plato's theories. The set of all mathmatical objects is variously called *Platonia* or the *Plenitude*. The Plenitude is Tegmark's level 4 parallel universe, and he argues that is no level 5 or higher.

Jürgen Schmidhuber introduced a different idea of the

---

[4]Tegmark uses *Multiverse* to refer to any ensemble of parallel universes — I prefer to stick to the convention that many others use that the Multiverse is the ensemble of many worlds arising from quantum mechanics.

Plenitude[111], by considering the output of a small computer program called a *universal dovetailer*, an idea first suggested by Bruno Marchal[93]. The dovetailer creates all possible programs (which are after all finite strings of computer instructions), and after creating each program runs a step of that program, and a step of each previously created program. In this way, the universal dovetailer executes all possible computer programs, which to a computationalist like Schmidhuber includes our universe amongst many other possible universes.

Now Schmidhuber supposes that there is a "Great Programmer", running the dovetailer on a "Great Computer", and that the Computer has the usual resource limitations of a Turing Machine[112]. This has some repercussions on the probability distribution of which string would be found if selected randomly. Simpler strings, with obvious patterns are far more likely than random string with no discernable pattern. This leads to some theoretical predictions, that can potentially be tested. Certain physical processes, such as radioactive decay, appear to be quite random. Whilst we can say with certainty that approximately half of the radioactive atoms in the material will have decayed over a period of time known as a *half life*, the sequence of times when the decays took place has no apparent pattern at all. However, in Schmidhuber's Plenitude, random descriptions are extremely unlikely, so seemingly random processes will be found to have an algorithmic description.

Clearly, there is a lot in common with Schmidhuber's Plenitude, and the Plenitude I proposed earlier, where each string is equally likely to be selected, the so called *uniform measure*. Whilst I'm philosophically uncomfortable with the notion of a "Great Computer" and its programmer, however the theory ought to be taken seriously.

Within the universal dovetailer's output is a description of a computer running another dovetailer, and so on ad infinitum. It is entirely possible that we do exist as a description within the output of a dovetailer, which itself may well be described in the output of another dovetailer. Since the theory makes some predictions about the likelihood of random sequences, this is potentially testable.

Paul Davies criticised such accounts of the Plenitude as leading to an infinite regress of creators and creatures[35]. There is indeed an infinite heirarchy of dovetailers creating plenitudes, however in Schmidhuber's case there is an ultimate "buck stops here" Great Programmer. In the version I propose, the Plenitude is simply the simplest possible object, equivalent to Nothing — no further explanation of Nothing's existence is needed. What is more crucial is that this infinite sequence of nested Plenitudes, all the same, can be summed over to obtain meaningful probabilities, and this does turn out to be the case.

Marchal uses the universal dovetailer in a somewhat different way to Schmidhuber. Marchal's Plenitude is *arithmetic Platonism*, that all properties of numbers are true independent of what you or I might think about them. Amongst mathematical structures, universal Turing machines exist, capable of running universal dovetailers. Along with the assumption that our minds can be copied, and perfectly simulated on some type of Turing machine, the appearance of a physical material reality experienced by the mind follows, without the need of a concrete computer running the dovetailer, nor is there any need for Schmidhuber's Great Programmer to exist. This is the *Universal Dovetailer Argument*, and is expressed most succinctly in [89].

There is also a strong connection between the Plenitude of bitstrings and Tegmark's Plenitude of mathematical objects. Mathematicians try to write down a minimal set of assumptions of the mathematical object they're studying, called *axioms*. The idea is that every theorem can be proved by application of logic to the axioms. For example, all the theorems in Euclid's *Geometry* can be derived from a set of 5 axioms. David Hilbert[64] had as one of his grand challenges the complete formalisation of all of mathematics as a minimal set of axioms from which all of mathematical knowledge can be derived. Alas for Hilbert, Kurt Gödel[56] demonstrated that arithmetic of integers cannot be axiomatised in this way — there will always be true theorems than can never be proved from any finite set of consistent axioms.

However, for any given set of axioms, in theory, one can enumerate over all possible theorems that can proved by that axiom set. If we consider these *finite axiomatic systems* to be the mathematical objects in Tegmark's Plenitude, rather than objects containing unprovable theorems, then each of these axioms sets will be found somewhere in Schmidhuber's bitstring Plenitude. Of course not all bitstrings correspond to mathematical objects, since they may describe inconsistent axiom sets. So we might say that Tegmark's Plenitude is a subset of Schmidhuber's one. Contrariwise, the theory of universal Turing machines is a mathematical theory, and a universal dovetailer is a formal specification. We can find Schmidhuber's Plenitude within Tegmark's!

It might seem from these considerations that Tegmark's Plenitude and Schmidhuber's Plenitudes are equivalent. However, this is not true. Schmidhuber's Plenitude is a *member* of Tegmark's, not a subset. We already knew that Schmidhuber's Plenitude is a member of itself, so this is not really all that surprising.

Tegmark doesn't actually say whether his ensemble consists of just the finite axiomatic systems (although this seems to be implied in his work), or whether he includes things like uncomputable objects or unprovable theorems also. I would like to point out that we observers can never access uncomputable things — we can only describe them, or give them labels. As an example of an uncomputable number, consider the probability that some reference universal Turing machine U will halt, given an arbitrary bitstring as input. The well known *Halting Theorem*[81, Lemma 1.7.5] states that no algorithm exists to determine which bitstrings will cause U to halt. Hence the halting probability, which is a rigourously definable number between 0 and 1, cannot be computed. I do not think it a loss to be able to describe things not in the Plenitude, in order to have a Plenitude with zero information, the simplest possible object.

Theories of parallel universes have become more fashionable in the last twenty years or so. Tegmark's level 1 universe is the least controversial – to disbelieve it would require believing that the universe suddenly changes its character just over the event horizon. Inflation has been successful in explaining various aspects of the universe such as its flatness, it homogeneity and its lack of topological defects. If inflation has happened once, it should have happened many times in different parts of spacetime. This leads naturally to Tegmark's level 2 parallel universe.

Even though the Multiverse of Wheeler and de Witt was first such parallel universes idea to be considered under the aegis of Physics, it has not received widespread support amongst practising physicists. However amongst cosmologists and string theorists, the opposite is true, and these people are the ones most likely to be consid-

ering the matter deeply. Frank Tipler cites a survey by
David Raub of "leading cosmologists and other quantum
field theorists" about the Many Worlds Interpretation,
and gives the following breakdown[137, 107]:

"Yes, I think MWI is true"	58%
"No, I don't accept MWI"	18%
"Maybe it's true but I'm not yet convinced"	13%
"I have no opinion one way or the other"	11%

Amongst the adherents were listed Stephen Hawking, Murray Gell-Mann and Richard Feynman.

My own personal conversion to the Many Worlds Interpretation occurred sometime in the early nineties. I
had always had difficulties with the main competing interpretations, the Copenhagen Interpretation, with its
instantaneous, universe-wide collapse of wave functions,
and of the Bohmian pilot wave theory, which was very
similar to the Many Worlds Interpretation, except that
one branch was singled out as *real* by a proposed *pilot wave*, the other branches remaining mere possibilities that never become actual. However, until the 1980s,
technology had not been able to handle single quantum
mechanical particles, real physical experiments involved
many particles that were easily described by the statistical distributions computed from quantum theory. It
was in particular, the experiments of Alain Aspect[6] that
convinced me interpretations of quantum mechanics were
necessary, and in Sherlock Holmes style, after eliminat-
ing the "impossible" (Copenhagen Interpretation, Bohm
Pilot-wave Interpretation etc.) whatever remained had
to be taken seriously.

In a later development of my thought, I realised that
the Copenhagen Interpretation is the Many World Interpretation "seen from the inside" (see §9.7).

Finally, to Tegmark's level 4 Plenitude. Whilst influenced strongly by Tegmark, and Schmidhuber, it was the neatness of the zero-information property of the Plenitude introduced above that converted me into being a latter day Platonist. Some scientists, including Deutsch, have argued that there is no physical evidence for parallel worlds beyond that of the level 3 Multiverse, and so it is pointless speculating on its existence. They are right, in a sense. As we will see later on in the book, observers must see themselves in a quantum mechanical world, by virtue of being observers. Other types of mathematical structure existing in Plato's Plenitude can never be observed, so in some sense are less *real* than observable structures. However as a complete explanation for the origin of everything, the Plenitude is required.

3.3 Spontaneous Symmetry Breaking

In some physical models, the equations used have a symmetry, yet the equilibrium state is not symmetric. The classic model of this type is *ferromagnestism*, which describes the physics in ordinary iron magnets. The system is symmetric, in that there is nothing different about the iron at the north pole of the magnet as the south, yet below a certain temperature, the so-called *Curie Temperature*, the magnet will spontaneously aquire a magentic field[5].

The Plenitude we introduced is symmetric — a fact is just as likely as its opposite. The process of observation induces a spontaneous symmtery breaking of the Plenitude (the possibilities) into observed facts (the actualities), since the whole plenitude (the symmetric state) is not observable. Many, many creation myths have the structure of some devine creator "splitting the void", of

---

[5]At least within individual domains of the material

creating an assymetry of some sort (eg see the Genesis quote that introduces this chapter). In spontaneous symmetry breaking, a creator is not needed, or rather, the observer takes the role of the creator.

Symmetry breaking turns out to be one of two fundamental physical principles that can explain why a particular value is observed — the other being the *anthropic principle*, which I will discuss in a later chapter. Symmetry breaking generates contingency, whereas the anthropic principle introduces necessity.

Chapter 4

A Theory of Observation

Pluralitas non est ponenda sine necessitate
Plurality should not be posited without necessity

William de Ockham

4.1 Occam's Razor

Occam's razor is generally attributed to William de Ockham (ca 1285–1349), and is not so much a physical principle, but a metaphysical one. In a situation where one is making a choice between two or more theories, each of which is compatible with the evidence collected to date, there should be no reason to prefer one theory over another. Yet Occam's razor, with its prescription for picking the simplest theory in some sense, will more often than not deliver the theory that is compatible with future experiments, yet the competing, and more complex theories end up being falsified by data.

Another metaphysical principle often applied in scientific theories is "beauty". Albert Einstein says:

> *"The creative scientist studies nature with the rapt gaze of the lover, and is guided as often by aesthetics as by rational considerations in guessing how nature works."*

Beauty is an emotional reaction on behalf of the scientist — good scientists will have a well developed intuition, or hunch about what is the most likely theory to work, out of the options thought up at the time. Beauty is often linked to simplicity, however — fewer parameters in a theory, or simpler looking equations for example.

In the 1960s, Solomonoff developed his ideas of algorithmic complexity as a way of addressing this mystery of why Occam's razor should be an effective principle. His work was followed up by Levi, who corrected several technical problems in Solomonoff's work. The result was the *Solomonoff-Levi* distribution, also known as the *Universal Prior*. Roughly speaking, the universal prior is the probability distribution $P(x) = \frac{\omega(x)}{2^L}$ introduced in §2.4, where $\omega(x)$ is the size of the equivalence class of programs running on a universal Turing machine that output the string x and stop. Since complexity is related via equation (2.1) to the logarithm of the universal prior, this result (and similar ones) is often called an *Occam's razor theorem*.

This prior explains why we a born into a simple world. The mind of a baby contains just enough information in order to bootstrap an understanding of the world about it. As we start observing the world, information is pouring into our senses. As we age, our mind develops as it makes sense of this new information, finding patterns, making theories so that the world of an adult human being is a fantastically rich and complex thing.

4.2 The White Rabbit Problem

This does however pose a problem. The universal prior explains why an individual world, or observer moment, is simple, but once time is introduced, why should the next observer moment bear any relation to its predecessor? Most bitstrings are purely random — there is no algorithm that can faithfully reproduce the string, save for one that contains a copy of the string within it. Why is it that the data streaming in through our sense has regularities that allow us to create theories? In short, why "the unreasonable effectiveness of mathematics"?[152]

This problem is called the *problem of induction* (induction being the process of deducing general rules from a sample of data), but is more poetically called the White Rabbit problem in a literary allusion to Lewis Carrol's *Alice in Wonderland.* In other forums, this problem goes by the more modern literary allusion of *Harry Potter world.* Simply stated, given the universe has always behaved in an orderly, law abiding fashion, what prevents the sudden appearance of a white rabbit, wearing a waistcoat and stopwatch, from flying through your bedroom window?

There are a few answers given to this problem — the first is that it is not really a problem at all, that physical reality is objective and described by a simple mathematical law that human kind in its ingenuity might hope to uncover. This position we might call *physicalism*, in the sense that Physicists usually assume an objective physical reality obeying a small set of pre-ordained physical laws, which they consider is their task to work out. Unfortunately this begs the question of where this simple mathematical rule might come from — short of supposing an unexplained deity placed it there, physicists holding to this view tend to assume that perhaps there is only one mathematical theory that consistently makes sense for reality, a final theory from which all else can be derived[146].

A subtle variation on this theme was recently promoted by Stephen Wolfram[153] in his book "A New Kind of Science". He assumes that physical law emerges out of the action of a simple mathematical rule called a cellular automaton. Scientists' task is to work out what is the CA rule generating our universe, and to explore the universes of nearby CAs. Exploring CAs just requires a computer albeit the more powerful the better, so according to Wolfram, we already have the tools to explore neighbouring universes, and other forms of life[29]. Unfortunately, the full space of CA possibilities is rather like Borges' Library of Babel — the task of establishing what are the interesting universes is well nigh impossible.

The notion that the universe might be some gigantic cellular automaton is not new with Wolfram — it dates back at least to Zuse in the 1960s[155], but Wolfram has made a lot of important contributions to the field of cellular automata.

Of course with this solution, one loses the previous explanation for why Occam's razor works. However, the problem of induction gets far worse once you admit existence to the Plenitude of all descriptions[75]. Whilst the Occam's razor theorem guarantees that a randomly picked string is more likely to be simple than complex, once we introduce time into the picture, the situation changes. At any point in time, we have observed a finite prefix of the chosen string, then continue the string by accreting bits to the end of it as further observations are performed. The newly acquired data is not constrained (as all infinite bit continuations are equally likely), so why then is induction so successful?

Jürgen Schmidhuber, introduced in chapter 3, sees a simple algorithm called a *universal dovetailer* generating the set of descriptions from which we see one of the sequences selected randomly. Since there must be a "Great Computer" on which the dovetailer algorithm is run, it turns out that simple descriptions are generated more rapidly than more complex ones. He introduces a new measure, which he calls the *speed prior* that reflects this process.[112] As a consequence, it is simply more likely that the universe's description will satisfy a simple algorithmic law, than for it to be completely random.

Even if there is no "Great Computer", but simply the all-descriptions Plenitude discussed in chapter 3, within this Plenitude exist descriptions of computers with bounded resources running universal dovetailers. Nothing prevents us from being in a simulation[22], which in turn is running in the Everything. So Schmidhuber has a point. Do infinite resource computers exist in the Plenitude? If so, then are infinite resource computers any more likely than finite ones. If not, then can conscious observers exist within a resource bounded simulation. This last question I will address in a later chapter. The speed prior does, however, make a specific prediction that can be tested. Supposed sources of randomness within the world will ultimately turn out to have an algorithmic description — they won't, in fact, be random at all.

The third approach, worked out by Alistair Malcolm and myself[85, 128, 84] acknowledges the fact that observers have been honed by millions of years of evolution to detect patterns — patterns that are essential for survival. This may be for avoiding predators, or for determining what is good to eat. It is obviously vital that animals are not confused by the presence of noise on their senses, for example caused by shadows. So observers will filter their inputs to more robustly obtain meaning from the data streaming in through their senses. What this implies is that around each short, algorithmic description are a bunch of quite random descriptions considered equivalent by the observer. So good is this signal processing system, that when humans are presented with random blobs of ink, as in a *Rorshach* test, they will frequently see objects or patterns within the blob of ink.

Of course, around simple descriptions are a larger number of equivalent random descriptions, than there are around more complex descriptions, with the number of equivalent descriptions exponentially decreasing with increasing complexity. Events such as flying white rabbits, or fire-breathing dragons appearing out of thin air are very complex and so are extremely unlikely to be observed. It might seem that the real world is complex too, with amazing creatures existing within complex ecosystems. However this complexity is actually the outcome of a very simple process called evolution, whereas miracles are much more complex as no simple process exists leading up to that miracle. Whilst random data appearing at our senses is very likely, the random part of the sequence is simply discarded as "noise". To an observer, one random bitstring is the same as any other, effectively having a null meaning, as discussed in §2.3. According to the complexity definition equation (2.1), our evolved observer will attribute very low complexity to random data[125].

Consequently the problem of induction is not a problem for the Plenitude, provided one of two scenarios exist. Either we are living in a simulation running on a computer with bounded resources, au Schmidhuber, or observers always tend to model reality, find patterns, theories and so on that compress the description of the world around them, discarding bits around the edge that don't fit the model as "noise" aux Standish/Malcolm.

Later (§9.4), I will argue that a source of randomness is in fact essential for an observer to function, as a consequence my preferred solution to the problem of induction is the one I worked out with Alistair Malcolm.

4.3 Time

In the previous section, we have snuck in an important concept with little discussion. We assumed that observers are embedded in something called *time*. Time is something quite mysterious. Unlike other space dimensions, our conscious selves appear to "flow through time". We talk about an observer being born into a world, a simple world, that progressively becomes more complex as observations are performed and the resulting information accreted.

Yet could we do without time? To observe a bit of information requires comparing two different things. These two things must be brought together to measure the difference. At very least we need a single topological dimension that separates things, and that the mind of the observer can focus its attention from one spot to another. As John A. Wheeler said:

> "Time is what prevents everything from happening at once."

This is a very minimal requirement of time, which can admit many models. It admits the conventional western/scientific model, which is of a 1D continuous linear space. It also admits more exotic alternatives such as cyclic time,[1] or a 1D manifold (called a *world line*) with

---

[1]Later the need for time to be *ordered* will become clear. Cyclic

a 4D Riemannian space — the view of time according to General Relativity.

Because the temporal dimension appears necessary in order compare things, and thus extract information from the environment, I postulate that all observers in the Plenitude must find themselves within a temporal dimension. This I call the *TIME postulate*.

General Relativity helps clarify the difference between this time we talk about, and the coordinate time that appears in equations of physics. Coordinate time is a set of dates when things happen. In General Relativity, the time coordinate is a fourth dimension of a space-time continuum. It behaves somewhat differently to the three dimensions of space that we're familiar with, by virtue of the *non-Euclidean* structure of space-time, nevertheless it is simply a coordinate in that space.

On the other hand, the world line can also be parametrised by a single number, called *proper time*. In the language of General Relativity, what we're talking about when we say time is proper time, in the observer's framework. However, because it is ultimately grounded on the observer, I will use the term *psychological time*.

So far, all the examples I've mentioned have been continuous. There are other alternatives, for instance *discrete time*, which is a popular alternative. Versions of string theory posit that there is a fundamental scale called *Planck time* (and Planck space), which limits how finely we can divide any interval. Computer simulations usually have discrete time, however it is assumed to approximate continuous time as the timestep is decreased towards zero.

A discrete set can be mapped to the set of integers,

---

time is not globally ordered, since A happens before B happens before A, but is locally ordered by cutting the loop at some point where the integer value is the index of the element within that set. Thinking of time as a set gives rise to many more possibilities. For example, the set of rational numbers, or numbers that can be expressed as a fraction or ratio of two integers. This set has the property of being dense in the continuum (ie a rational number can be found arbitrarily close to a randomly picked real number), but also of measure zero (there are vastly more irrational numbers than rational ones).

Another measure of dimension is the *Hausdorff dimension*, sometimes also known as *fractal dimension*. The Hausdorff dimension of the set of rational numbers is zero, whilst the topological dimension is one. For an arbitrary set, the Hausdorff dimension is a real number less than or equal to that set's topological dimension[58]. An example set with Hausdorff dimension $\frac{\ln 2}{\ln 3} \approx 0.6309$ is the *Cantor set*, which can be constructed by taking the line segment [0,1], and removing the middle third. Then repeat this operation on the two remaining line segments. See Fig 4.1. Sets with non-integral Hausdorff dimension are commonly called *fractals*[88]. These sets are also candidates for time.

The theory of *time scales*[17] gives a way of handling the different possibilities for time. Time scales in Bohner and Peterson's book are closed subsets of the real line, including discrete sets of points, including the limit points if infinite, rational numbers, cantor sets as well as continuous line segments. [2]

---

[2]For our time notion, I propose something a little more basic, that is time is simply a set with an ordering.

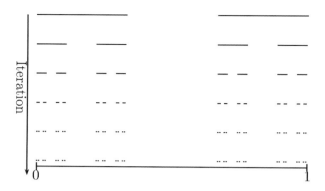

Figure 4.1: Constructing the Cantor set

4.4   Observer Moments

In subsequent chapters of this book, and in many of the
discussions on the Everything list, the notion of *observer
moment* is often employed. The notion is perhaps not
sufficiently precise, as occasionally the list will lapse into
navel gazing exercises to attempt to define the term.

Nick Bostrom introduced the notion of observer moment in his PhD thesis[20, 21], and used it to define
the *strong self sampling assumption.* We will discuss
Bostrom's *self sampling assumption* in chapter 5.1, so will
postpone further discussion of that principle until then.

To make matters more precise, we found in §4.1 that
observers are selecting descriptions, and reading and interpreting a finite number of bits from the description.
Then with the TIME postulate, we are assuming that the
observer is repeating the process, updating er worldview,
and updating the interpretation applied to the description also. Each such update is a discrete step, defined by
the set of all descriptions that map to the observer's current worldview. Such a set of descriptions we can call the

observer moment. Equivalently, we could use the dual of this concept, and say an observer moment is the set of constraints defining this set of descriptions (i.e. the observers "current state of knowledge"). Part of the reason for using so many different terms is to make contact with objects in different theories. Another term often used informally to mean observer moment is *world* (as in Many Worlds Interpretation), or *universe*, provided it is clear one is not talking about a *history*, which is a sequence of observer moments.

From an observer's point of view, observer moments form a discrete set, in a well defined order. One can choose a map (or mathematical function) from this sequence of observer moments to the set of real numbers *that preserves the ordering.* Certain physical processes perform this mapping in a uniform and consistent way, independent of the observer (eg the pendulum, or oscillations of electromagnetic radiation). This mapping defines a *clock.*

One of the recurring debates about observer moments is whether they are instantaneous (an infinitesimal "moment"), or whether they have finite duration. Whilst this debate presupposes a notion of physical time (which I do not want to preempt), I will comment that observer moments do have finite duration, in the sense that each observer moment is discrete, and the value of any clock will differ between any two observer moments by a finite amount.

4.5 Measure

Along with observer moments, we need the concept of *measure.* Measure is a a function μ defined over sets satisfying an additivity property:

$$\mu(A \cup B) = \mu(A) + \mu(B) - \mu(A \cap B) \qquad (4.1)$$
$$\mu(\emptyset) = 0 \qquad (4.2)$$

where $\cup$ and $\cap$ are the usual set operations of union and intersection, and $\emptyset$ is the empty set[31]. A *probability* is then a measure that takes a value in the range $[0, 1]$.

For example, the uniform measure attaches equal weights to each point of a set. To measure the size of a set of observers having property A, one integrates over all observers having that property using a uniform measure.

Probability is a measure whose integral over all sets[3] adds up to one. If a real-valued measure integrates to a finite positive value m, it can be *normalised* to a probability by dividing by m. A uniform measure is only a probability if the measure is restricted to sets whose measure is bounded, line segments for example, but not the real line.

Measure has been often discussed on the Everything list, as it is crucial to understanding anthropic reasoning arguments. Usually, measure is taken to be positive in these discussions, even if not actually normalisable (eg the uniform measure over the real line). Some people think that complex measures are the most general type of measure[31], where μ can take arbitrary complex values. However, it turns out that most general type of measure is actually what is called a *spectral measure*, where the measure function μ is defined over a *Banach* space. Banach spaces are a type of vector space where the vectors have length (ie are *normed*). Examples include the

---

[3]Mathematicians call the union of all sets to be measured the *domain* of the measure

real numbers, Euclidean vector spaces such as our familiar 3D space, and so on. I will show in Appendix C how one can infer likely outcomes from these more general measures. In the derivation of quantum mechanics given in appendix D, however, the most general measure for selecting observers is a complex measure.

4.6 Functionalism

Functionalism is in essence the the assumption that "man is machine". More explicitly, if one can build a machine that simulates our brains sufficiently accurately, and we can simulate our environment sufficiently accurately, "I" could not tell whether my mind was instantiated on a real brain, or exists within a simulation. Furthermore, there is a kind of degeneracy between the real brain and a sufficiently realistic simulation. Moreover I cannot tell whether my next observer moment is instantiated on a real brain or in a virtual one.

Functionalism contrasts absolutely with certain theological notions of an immortal "soul" that exists independently of the body. In this book, I take functionalism as a given, without further debate or justification. As we shall see in chapter 8, functionalism is sufficient to predict an immortal existence of the mind, without the need of an independent "soul".

Functionalism implies *supervenience*. If a similar enough arrangement of functionally equivalent parts is sufficient to produce the same mind, it follows that a different mind can only exist with a functionally different arrangement of parts. This latter doctrine is known as supervenience[4].

---

[4]Note that Bruno Marchal equates supervenience (or at least "physical supervenience") with what I have previously described as

One particular fact about functionalism is important — it is possible to make a copy of your mind. Bruno Marchal calls this the "Yes Doctor" postulate: consider a situation of being informed that you have inoperable brain cancer, and that the only possible cure is a brain transplant with a mechanical brain. If you say "yes, Doctor", it means you believe it is in fact possible to copy your mind in this way.

Arthur Dent, from Hitchhiker's Guide to the Galaxy is quite obviously from the "No Doctor" camp: As Douglas Adams writes about Arthur Dent's brain:

> "It could always be replaced," said Benji reasonably, "if you think it's important."
>
> "Yes, an electronic brain," said Frankie, "a simple one would suffice."
>
> "A simple one!" wailed Arthur.
>
> "Yeah," said Zaphod with a sudden evil grin, "you'd just have to program it to say What? and I don't understand and Where's the tea? - who'd know the difference?"
>
> "What?" cried Arthur, backing away still further.
>
> "See what I mean?" said Zaphod and howled with pain because of something that Trillian did at that moment.
>
> "I'd notice the difference," said Arthur.
>
> "No you wouldn't," said Frankie mouse, "you'd be programmed not to."

---

physicalism. So when Bruno says that computationalism contradicts physical supervenience, he really means that it contradicts the necessity for a concrete physical universe to implement a mind.

Computationalism, which we will come to next, is a particular form of functionalism, in which the conscious being is logically equivalent to a Turing machine.

4.7 Computationalism

Artificial Intelligence (AI) is a domain of computer science that aims to make intelligent machines, and ultimately conscious machines. The *weak artificial intelligence* thesis is that this is indeed possible.

Computationalism, also sometimes known as the *strong AI* thesis, is the belief that any conscious being is capable of being simulated on a computer. Clearly strong AI implies weak AI.

Remember to computer scientists, the term *machine* is quite specific. A machine can be represented exactly by a Turing machine, which as mentioned in chapter 3 is a precise, formal mathematical object. Whilst real computers are often thought of as universal Turing machines (ie Turing machines that can be programmed to emulate any other Turing machine), they actually differ from universal Turing machines in a couple of important ways. The first way is that Turing machines have access to an infinite amount of storage in the form of its tape, whereas computers in practice have only a finite amount. Imagine, if you will, that your desktop PC occasionally pauses, displaying the message "insert new hard disk to continue". A physical implementation of a Turing machine would have to do something like this, and perhaps also occasionally print the message "Press F1 to boot new universe"!

The second difference is access to true random numbers. It is widely believed (Schmidhuber excepted! see §3.2) that decay of radioactive atoms occur at completely unpredictable times, although on average the distribution of decay events follows a well defined Poisson law. One can easily attach a Geiger counter with a radioactive source to one of the computer's input ports, and hey presto, you have a machine capable of computing genuinely random strings, something a Turing machine by definition is incapable of doing. Actually it is not even necessary to attach a Geiger counter to your computer — since your computer is interacting with humans via input devices of some kind, such as keyboards and mice, the computer's processor is constantly being interrupted as you press the keys or move the mouse. Each interruption introduces an unpredictable time delay to it operation, which can be collected and presented as a series of truly random numbers. On Linux computers, there is a "file"[5] called `/dev/random` that you can read these random numbers from. This concept has been extended in software called HAVEGE[116] to maximise the amount of random information that can be extracted from modern computer processors, such as the Intel Pentium 4.

Anyway, true computationalism demands that consciousness be completely emulated by a Turing machine. I shall argue later that randomness appears to be a necessary ingredient of creative thought. This implies that if our minds are computations, we cannot observe the computer on which our mind runs. Instead our brains (the "machines" upon which our minds supervene) must necessarily be non-deterministic, so I have sometimes considered myself to be a non-computationalist. However Bruno Marchal provides an interpretation of computationalism that not only allows for this subjective indeterminism, but indeed requires it.

A related concept to computationalism is the *Church-*

---

[5]It is not really a file, but a "pretend" file called a *device*

Turing thesis. Strictly speaking, the Church-Turing thesis is a definition: Any *effective algorithm* can be performed by a Turing machine. This has more to say about what precisely we mean by computation in a formal sense, than limits to computations in general. The field of *hypercomputation*[102] opens up the logical possibility of computers with greater computational power than the class of Turing machines. It then becomes an open question as to whether such *hypercomputers* can be instantiated in the physical world we live in. The hypothesis that the world we live in is equivalent to a computation running on some Turing machine is called the *strong Church-Turing thesis.* A weaker version of this thesis called the *Physical Church-Turing thesis* is that any physically computable function can be computed by a Turing machine. Since conscious thought is a physical process, (pace Descartes), the Physical Church-Turing thesis implies computationalism.

I think the Physical Church-Turing thesis (and consequently the strong Church-Turing thesis) is disproven, in that measurement of quantum systems generates random sequences of results. This is a widely assumed consequence of quantum mechanics, and indeed the many worlds interpretation leaves no doubt that each observer will see a world selected at random from the Multiverse. A more recent claim of the invalidity of the Physical Church-Turing thesis, based on the phenomenon of Brownian motion, not quantum theory is made by Petrus Potgieter[106], based on work by Willem Fouché[50]. However Fouché himself makes no such claim in his paper, instead what he has shown is that the *mathematical model* of Brownian motion, the so-called *Wiener process* is algorithmically random. Real Brownian systems are expected to diverge from the Wiener description at some level —

for example at the molecular level, where the Brownian particles are interacting with individual atoms via intermolecular forces.

Nevertheless, these theses may be rescued for the Multiverse as a whole, which is deterministic, with its time evolution described by the Schrödinger equation. This is most clear for the case of a universe with a discrete number of states, and discrete time, and a Hamiltonian operator with rational coefficients. A computer can compute the exact history of the Multiverse from the associated discrete Schrödinger equation.

Bruno Marchal demonstrates that *computationalism* necessarily implies that the subjective experience of an observer is indeterminate[94, 95, 89]. All that is really needed to make the argument work is the "Yes Doctor" assumption. Bruno proposes a thought experiment whereby your brain, and indeed your body is destroyed within a "teleporter" in Brussels, and recreated in both Washington and Moscow. What do you experience? If computationalism is true, you cannot say that you experience nothing, nor does it make any sense to say you experience both Washington and Moscow. Therefore you must experience being transported to either Washington or Moscow, which one being indeterminate.

The trick is to realise that what you experience is a subjective, *first person* experience, whereas to an external observer sees a copy of you created at both Washington and Moscow, the objective, or *third person experience.* Max Tegmark uses the term *frog perspective* to refer to this first person experience, and the term *bird perspective* to refer to the third person experience[134]. Both perspectives are equally valid descriptors of reality, and one perspective need not be reducible to the other — i.e. the frog perspective may contain information and concepts such as the mind not directly representable in the bird perspective. This is another example of the general notion of emergence introduced in chapter 2 — the first person experience is emergent from the third.

Marchal's argument is really quite general. He is agnostic about the level of substitution needed to ensure the survival of your personal identity. It may, for example, be a simulation of the entire multiverse, of which your consciousness is but one tiny speck.

On the topic of computationalism, Tim Maudlin[96] wrote an influential paper using the characters of Olympia and Klara inspired by E. T. A. Hoffmann's *Der Sandmann*[6]. Marchal independently developed an equivalent argument called the *filmed graph* argument[92]. Olympia is a simple machine that replays a tape recording of the actions of a conscious being called Klara. Its behaviour is *indistinguishable* from that of Klara, given this exact sequence of environmental inputs. In 1950, Alan Turing[138] argued that if we could not distinguish between a computer running an artificial intelligence program, and a human being, then we must accept the machine as being conscious.

We would never accept that Olympia is conscious, she is far too simple a machine. The most obvious criticism is to ask about *counterfactuals*, the what-if questions. We could ask what if the environment differed from that of the recording? Clearly Olympia would start to diverge from the behaviour of Klara, and we could tell her apart from the real thing. However, let us suppose for the sake

---

[6]Hoffmann's tale does not directly touch upon the subject of Maudlin's paradox, but rather more generally on the consequences of automata capable of fooling people into believing the automata are real people. Hoffmann's spelling differs from Maudlin's also using Olimpia for Olympia, and Clara for Klara. Here we will use Maudlin's spelling.

of argument we are running a simulation with a precisely determined history. This simulation contains some conscious programs, as well as some programs that replay recordings like Olympia. Since the environment is completely predetermined, the counterfactuals never actually happen. Since we've assumed computationalism, we can make as many copies of Klara as there are timesteps in the simulation. Each copy of Klara is run to a different timestep i, and then stopped. In Maudlin's paper, Klara is perhaps an enormous clockwork machine, and can be stopped by placing a block of wood between the gears. Now the ith Klara is attached to Olympia so that *if* the environment differed from the original tape at timestep i, the block of wood is released, and that copy of Klara takes over from Olympia. Now, this augmented machine behaves as the original Klara would in any counterfactual situation. Yet all the copies of Klara are inert — since the environmental tape never differs from the original. How can the presence, or absence of consciousness depend on machinery which never operates?

We've stated this argument is terms of a simulation, however it applies equally well if we live in a deterministic world, where history has been preordained from the beginning of time.

Whilst Maudlin concluded that this argument was necessarily fatal for computationalism, Bruno Marchal provides a very different interpretation, based on his argument of the *filmed graph*[92, 94]. According to Marchal, computationalism is *necessarily* incompatible with the notion that a physical computer is needed to implement the conscious mind. Instead, abstract Platonic computations suffice.

My own interpretation of Maudlin's argument, and Marchal's filmed graph argument is slightly different. The argument implies the necessary existence of counterfactual realities, or more precisely, the counterfactual realities have exactly the same ontological status as the factual one — in other words the many worlds interpretation, or similar, and an indeterminate first person experience. For considering the Multiverse as a whole, only in one world history does Olympia successfully mimic Klara, in all the others she is shown up to be the sham she is. Indeterminate subjective experience, and many worlds is essential to the phenomenon of consciousness.

Some authors have suggested that quantum mechanics is integral to the phenomenon of consciousness, and that perhaps minds function as a *quantum computer.* [7] Roger Penrose is perhaps the leading proponent of this point of view[105]. Other people include Michael Lockwood[83] and Henry Stapp[129], although Stapp does not explicitly view the mind as a quantum computer, but considers the mind to be intimately involved with *wavefunction collapse.* Max Tegmark analysed Roger Penrose's suggestion for quantum computing in the brain, and concluded that any quantum coherence (needed for practical quantum computation) decays many orders of magnitude faster than the timescale on which neurons fire[135].

---

[7] Quantum computers are computational devices exploiting quantum superpositions to perform computations at astronomically greater speeds than is possible on classical computers. A loose interpretation of a quantum computer is a computer that exploits the parallel universes of the Multiverse to perform the computations in parallel. Quantum computing is an active area of research, and small quantum computers have been exhibited in the lab that hardly compete against conventional computers. Nevertheless, there doesn't appear to be any theoretical obstacles preventing quantum computers from achieving enormous computational speeds. David Deutsch has suggested that a quantum computation exceeding the capability of a classical computer employing the entire universe's resources is proof that the Multiverse idea is correct.

Lockwood preempted this criticism, and suggested that the brain may find itself in a *Bose-condensed* state analogous to superconductivity. He argues that this explains the Cartesian unity of consciousness arising from the distributed nature of the brain's architecture. He seems unaware that coherent phenomena can also arise in purely classical systems existing at a state of criticality. It seems more plausible to me that the unity of consciousness may be due to *self-organised criticality*[8] in the brain, operating under purely classical dynamics, than due to quantum effects. Rather, quantum effects may only be harnessed by the brain as a source of genuine random numbers, a theme that will be touched upon in the following chapters.

Marchal's *Universal Dovetailer Argument* [89] is an explicit series of thought experiments that lead to a startling set of conclusions (assuming computationalism as a working hypothesis).

1. Your next experience can be any consistent extension of your current. For example, if you are scanned, and a copy of yourself is created on the other side of the world, possibly with a delay, then you are just as likely to experience teleportation as staying home.

2. A sufficiently powerful simulation is just as likely to be your next experience as the real thing. Indeed, Nick Bostrom asks the question: "Are you living in a computer simulation?"[22].

3. Since Maudlin's argument indicates that a computational consciousness can supervene on effectively stationary machinery, there is no need for a concrete physical reality at all.

In this book, I propose a Plenitude of all descriptions, containing at least one that *is* a conscious observer. At first blush this seems strange, it looks like a category error — confusing mere description with the real thing, confusing the map with the territory. However, this is the only way of closing the ontology, otherwise there is forever something else breathing "fire into our equations" as Stephen Hawking put it. It should be treated as a working hypothesis until either it is demonstrated as clearly false, or a more detailed theory of conscious tells us how consciousness comes about. Furthermore, as I shall argue in the next section, the Anthropic Principle is completely mysterious, unless the observer is the description.

The interesting thing about Marchal's argument is that it shows that if computationalism is true, these other assumptions of mine are true. Computationalism can be considered a consistent model for descriptions to be self aware.

Chapter 5

Anthropic Reasoning

> All things physical are information-theoretic
> in origin and this is a participatory uni-
> verse...Observer participancy gives rise to
> information; and information gives rise to
> physics.
>
> *John A. Wheeler* [150]

5.1 Anthropic Principle

We, as observers, are part of this universe. Therefore, the
universe cannot have any property that contradicts our
existence. To the extent that our existence constrains the
form of the universe, we seem to have a causative role in
shaping the universe. This is known as the *Anthropic
Principle*[11].

This might have little significance, if it weren't for
a series of remarkable coincidences in physical parameters of the universe, such as the fine structure constant,
the ratio of proton to electron mass and the strengths
of the fundamental forces. If any of these parameters
were slightly different from their actual values, life as we

know it would be impossible[134]. The universe appears to exist on a "knife edge" in parameter space where life is possible. This cries out for an explanation. The three possible explanations are:

1. That the universe was constructed by a divine being, who had no choice but to design it in such a way as to harbour life.

2. That there is some physical principle (currently unknown). explaining why these fundamental constants have the values they do

3. We live in an ensemble of universes, each with different values of these parameters. Clearly, we will observe parameters compatible with life.

Given the philosophical stance of this book, it is not surprising that the third explanation is my preferred one.

The Anthropic Principle is not just a philosophical curiosity, but has actually been deployed to generate scientifically testable hypotheses, usually in cosmology. Perhaps the most famous example was Fred Hoyle's prediction of a specific resonance in the carbon nucleus, before this was experimentally measured, based on the reasoning that if this resonance didn't exist, elements heavier than Beryllium (the fourth element in the periodic table) could not have been made[67]. Another example closer in time and space to me is Charlie Lineweaver (who I know personally) using anthropic arguments to estimate the distribution of earth-like planets in the universe[82]. His predictions should be testable within the next few decades, as more and more extra-solar planets are discovered[113].

Whilst in one sense the Anthropic Principle seems obvious, it is actually profoundly mysterious. There is no doubt that the Anthropic Principle works, and it has passed all experimental tests to date. However, one could imagine being born into a virtual reality simulator, in the style of the movie *Matrix*, such that you had no knowledge whatsoever of the outside world containing your body[1], nor there being any representation of your body within the reality simulated by the simulator. In this case, observed reality is not constrained to be compatible with your existence. The Anthropic Principle will not apply in such worlds.

By reason of the Occam's razor theorem §4.1, we should be born into the simplest possible world, a world that would be utterly boring and lifeless. The Anthropic Principle prevents this catastrophe (which I call the *Occam catastrophe*) by requiring that the world be sufficiently complex to support conscious life. Clearly the Anthropic Principle is necessary, but why?

David Deutsch[43] argues an observer trapped within such a virtual reality would eventually notice inconsistencies in how that reality operates, and thus deduce the existence of a larger reality within which the observer is actually situated. John Barrow makes a similar point in his New Scientist article *Glitch!*[10], as does Daniel Dennett in *Consciousness Explained*[41]. Considering the case of a virtual reality which does not contain the observer, one in which there is no supervenience of the mind on any physical thing, just how might the observer deduce the e was really in a larger invisible external reality?

The only answer it seems to me is self awareness. Descartes said "I think, therefore I am". From being aware of one's own mind, one can deduce the existence of something outside of the impoverished virtual reality of one's experience, be it an immaterial mind, or an ac-

---

[1]We might imagine that a "shunt" was placed in your spinal column so that no proprioceptive sensations is received by your brain

tual brain for that mind to supervene, assuming supervenience.

We may therefore postulate that self-awareness is a necessary property of consciousness. This is a prediction, potentially falsifiable in the event of a fuller theory of consciousness being developed.

5.2   Doomsday Argument

An important example of anthropic reasoning is the so-called *Doomsday Argument*[77]. Consider listing all human beings that have ever lived, and the ones to be born in the future in birth order. Your *birth rank* is your position in this list. All else being equal, our birth rank should be typical, somewhere in the middle out of all humans that have lived, and will live in the future. We don't expect to be near either the beginning of the list, nor near the end. We currently live in a time of rapid population growth — if this were to continue, for example if humanity were leave the Earth and colonise the Galaxy, then we would find our birth rank to be amongst the earliest of all humans. Even if the population level was to stabilise for an extended period of time, the most typical birth should occur somewhere during this stable period, not during a period of exponential growth. The only remaining possibility is that of a dramatic population decline in the near future, either through natural demographic means[2], or through a catastrophic process (the "doomsday" of the argument's title).

This form of the argument is due to Richard Gott

---

[2]Recent UN demographics projections have recently revised downwards the population growth estimates over the next century, and are even predicting an absolute peak in human population by around the middle of this century[140].

III[70], who discovered the argument independently of Brandon Carter and John Leslie, who have written most prolificly on the subject. Gott's version is easier to explain to a nontechnical audience than Leslie's explanation, which involves the use of Bayesian statistics. Nick Bostrom's PhD thesis[20] examines this argument in great technical detail, and he provides an accessible summary on his website[3]. He introduces the concept of the *Self Sampling Assumption* (SSA), which provides another method of expressing the Doomsday argument[20, 21].

> Every observer should reason as if they were
> a random sample drawn from the set of all
> observers. *Self Sampling Assumption*

An application of this assumption can be seen in Fig. 5.1. The curves represent the population of observers as a function of time. The SSA converts these curves into a probability distribution of being born within a particular time interval. Clearly, the probability of being born in a period of rapid growth well before peak population levels is very low compared with the probability of being born somewhere near the peak. This is the essence of the Doomsday Argument.

Of course there are some alternative interpretations of the Doomsday Argument:

- There are an infinite total number of observers, which contradicts the DA's assumption of a finite list. The bottom scenario of Fig. 5.1 could be interpreted as the initial segment of a universe with an infinite number of observers, and it is clear we are not living in such a universe. However, an equally

---

[3]http://www.anthropic-principle.com

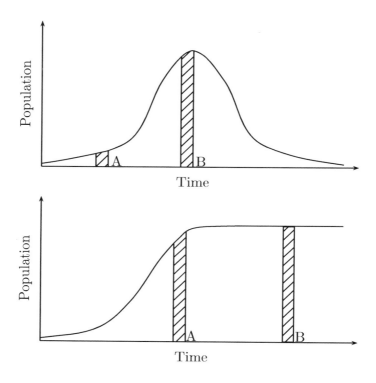

Figure 5.1: Two possible scenarios for population sizes into the future. In the top scenario, population grows to a peak, then plummets shortly afterwards. The most likely time to born is near the peak (eg at B), rather than away from the peak at A. In the bottom scenario, population stabilises at some level. The typical time to be born is during the stable population level at B, rather than during a period of massive growth at A. Knowing that populations levels are currently growing, leads one to conclude that we are living in the top scenario, somewhere near the peak, and that population sizes will shortly plummet.

possible scenario is that population growth continues forever (implying that the universe lasts forever), in which case we should not be surprised
to find ourselves in a period of rapid population
growth. In this scenario, we should expect that
past population levels should also have been growing, whereas in fact population levels were relatively
static for several thousands of years prior to the in-
dustrial revolution (see Fig. 5.2).

- There are extra-terrestrial observers. This would
  invalidate the doomsday argument based on birth
  rank. However, using Bostrom's SSA, we can conclude that extraterrestrial populations must be relatively insignificant in size, and so can be ignored,
  or similar size to our own population and growing
  in the same way, in which case the Doomsday argument applies equally to their population as it does
  to ours.

- That in the near future, humans will evolve into
  different entities (*posthuman*) that do not form part
  of the *reference class* of observers the SSA is applicable to. This could be in the form of uploading
  our conscious mind into a simulation, as suggested
  by Hans Morovic in *Mind Children*[101]. See also
  the essay *Staring into the Singularity*[154]. Posthuman could also refer to machines (such as robots)
  competing with humans and ultimately causing the
  extinction of *homo sapiens*. This is a frightening
  possibility. If this posthuman entity is not included
  in the SSA reference class, then these posthuman
  entities cannot be conscious. I would prefer to consider the possibility that in the future, posthuman
  minds are interlinked, and form part of a single,

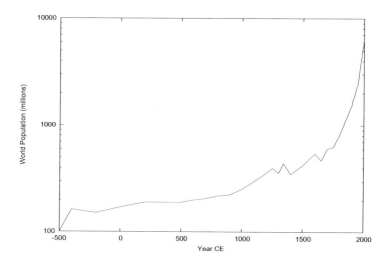

Figure 5.2: World population from 500 BCE to present. Data extracted from [141, 139]

or few superintelligent consciousnesses, rather than the many billions of independent consciousnesses currently occupying this planet.

- We are living in a Multiverse, and something like the *Quantum Theory of Immortality* (see chapter 8) holds. Basically the Doomsday still happens, but we never experience it, or we only experience the milder scenarios compatible with personal survival. This allows our future experience to include rising population levels[78]. Related to this issue, the MWI appears to resolve certain paradoxes that a hypothetical "Adam" (first human being) would experience in using the SSA[19].

Just how soon is this doomsday likely to be? Surprisingly, even with the heavy mathematical analysis usually applied to his subject, very few estimates of just how much time is left for our species is given. Bostrom gives a figure of 1200 years in his thesis[20], but it is a rather incidental analysis. In appendix B I analyse a worst-case scenario of populations continuing to grow at present rates until a catastrophic collapse of the population occurs. The time remaining until doomsday is just over a century. Whilst alarming, one should bear in mind that already population growth is slowing, and best estimates put population as peaking around 2050. This would postpone and draw out doomsday. Human history may last for a million years, but only at drastically reduced population levels from today's.

5.3   Anthropic Selection

We have already mentioned the principle of *symmetry breaking* (§3.3) as a causative explanation for a *contingent* property, and extended via the Occam's razor theorem. The *Anthropic Principle* introduced in this chapter is a causative explanation for a *necessary* property. At this point I'd like to introduce a major thesis of this book: Symmetry Breaking and the Anthropic Principle together suffice to explain all that there is. The *self sampling assumption* bridges the Anthropic Principle and Symmetry Breaking by updating the prior probability distribution obtained from the Occam's Razor theorem to include observer dependent selection effects, and then selecting randomly from the set of possibilities according to new distribution. This selection we will call *anthropic selection*.

5.4   Ants are not conscious

We can also use the Doomsday argument to investigate the consciousness of simple creatures like ants, or amoebae. There are vastly more ants than there are human beings, so if ants were conscious, it would be rather surprising to *be* a human being.

This is, of course, a rather dubious argument. When we humans say "ants", we mean an individual of thousands of different species of organism — it is a little unfair to compare a whole order of insects with a single species. Yet even the classification of species seems a little arbitrary for applying anthropic arguments. Consider the following argument, which has the same structure as before. China has over a billion people, however you, dear reader, are more likely to be an inhabitant of an English speaking country with a population far less than China's, given my choice of language for this book. I happen to live in Australia, for instance, a country with around 1/50th the population of China. It would be absurd to conclude that Chinese people are unconscious, so what went wrong?

We can rephrase the Chinese question in a different way: *What is the expected population size of one's country of birth?* It turns out (see Fig 5.3) that there are far more countries with fewer people, than countries with more people. The precise relationship is the number of countries is proportional to $1/x$, where x is the population of the country. This law is an example of Zipf's law, and it appears in all sorts of circumstances, for example the distribution of lengths of sticks that have been snapped in half, or the frequency with which words are used in the English language. It is a general feature of a classification system that is arbitrary.

With Zipf's law, the number of countries of a given

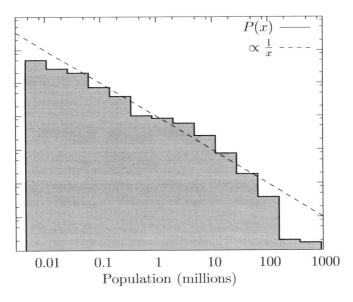

Figure 5.3: Distribution of national populations in the year 2000, plotted on a log-log scale. US Census Bureau data[142]

population size exactly offsets the population of those countries, so anthropically speaking, we should expect to find ourselves in just about any country, with the same probability. Being Australian is no more surprising than being American or Chinese.

OK, well lets get back to our ants. More than likely, the distribution of species populations also follows Zipf's law, so it is no surprise to find ourselves being any particular species. However, let us ask a different question: "what is our expected body mass if we are randomly sampled from the reference class of conscious beings?". Let us further restrict our attention to those conscious beings living on the Earth. Assume a probability distribution $P(m)$ of body masses over the class of conscious beings, and divide the mass axis up into mass classes $M_i \leq m < M_{i+1}$. There must be a minimum mass M_0 such that the mass any conscious being is greater than M_0[4]. There may also be a limit to the maximum mass for an organism — certainly the largest plants and animals operate near their physiological limits. For $P(m)$ to be a probability distribution, either there is a maximum mass limit, or $P(m)$ decays faster than m^{-1}, as $m \to \infty$.

Given we're interested in comparing ants and humans, mass ranges over multiple orders of magnitude, so the mass classes should be chosen exponentially, ie $M_i = \mu M_{i-1} = \mu^i M_0$.

The probability of finding our body mass in the mass class $[M_i, M_{i+1})$ is given by the integral of the probability distribution over that mass range, i.e.

$$P(m \in [M_i, M_{i+1}) \quad = \quad \int_{M_i}^{M_{i+1}} P(m')dm'$$

---

[4]The smallest known bacteria is around 200nm, and all viruses are bigger than about 20nm, so all living things will have a mass greater than 10^{-17}g (10 attograms).

$$\approx \quad P(\sqrt{\mu}M_i)M_i(\mu - 1) \quad (5.1)$$

What happens next depends on exactly what form $P(m)$ takes. If $P(m)$ decays faster than m^{-1}, the probability
$P(m \in [M_i, M_{i+1}))$ also decays as $m \to \infty$. A random sampling of this distribution will most likely pick a mass near the peak of $P(m)$ (if one exists), or near the minimum possible mass for consciousness if $P(m)$ is monotonic. Alternatively, if $P(m)$ decays slower than m^{-1}, then the maximum possible mass is more likely.

There is a well known biological law (called Damuth's law)[34] that states the population density of a species is inversely proportional to the 3/4ths power of that species' body mass, *i.e.* $d \propto m^{-3/4}$. To turn this result into the mass distribution of individuals $P(m)$, we need to multiply this law by the mass distribution of species $S(m)$. Informally, we note that there are many more smaller bodied species of animals than larger ones; there are many more types of insect than of mammals, for example. The exact form of the distribution function $S(m)$ is still a matter of conjecture. Theoretical models suggest that $S(m)$ is peaked at intermediate body sizes[69], and experimental results appear to confirm this[118]. The speciosity peak for animals appears to be within the domain of insects[5], or possibly even smaller as some recent research into nematode diversity on the deep sea floor indicates[104].

Nevertheless, when speciosity is multiplied by Damuth's law, $P(m)$ falls off much faster than m^{-1}, and so we should not expect to have a body mass much higher than insects, unless such animals are not conscious. An-

---

[5]Beetles are renowned for their diversity of forms. The well-known British scientist J.B.S. Haldane was once asked by a cleric what his study of life told him about God, he replied that "God had an inordinate love of beetles".

thropic reasoning leads us to expect that our body mass should be around the minimum possible value for conscious creatures.

Having shown that individual ants are not conscious (to the extent that anthropic arguments are believable), consider the thought provoking suggestion of Douglas Hofstadter that perhaps ant nests as a whole are conscious[66]. Ants are known to communicate by means of exchanging pheromones, and self-organised patterns and behaviour emerges from the myriad of interchanges between individual ants. Perhaps, like the human brain being composed of neurons that are individually not conscious, the collective activity of a nest of ants instantiates conscious behaviour. It is a beguiling concept, that is not easy to dismiss. From an anthropic perspective, the number of ant nests are unlikely to outnumber the number of human beings by a huge amount.

5.5   Mirror Tests

In §5.1, I argue that *self awareness* is a necessary property of consciousness. Gordon Gallup developed the *mirror test* as a means of assessing whether nonhuman animals are self-aware. The basic idea is simple: paint an odourless spot somewhere on the animal's body, place a mirror in front of the animal, and observe the animal to see whether it reacts in a way consistent with it being aware the spot is located on its body.

Not many animals are known to have passed the mirror test. Only chimpanzees, bonobos, orangutans, bottlenose dolphins and humans older than about three years of age are known to pass the mirror test. Surprisingly, gorillas don't, although one specific gorilla has, Koko. Koko is famous for being able to "talk" — in American sign language.

Of course the mirror test can be criticised that it favours animals who rely on vision. For many mammals, other senses, such as the sense of smell, or of hearing are more important. This might be the case with dogs, who do not pass the mirror test, but seem conscious to many people. Dogs rely far more on olfactory ability than visual. However the rarity of animals that pass the mirror test indicates the rarity of self-awareness, and of consciousness in the animal kingdom. If these other species, apes, dolphins etc. are conscious, we humans still outnumber them manyfold, so anthropically speaking it is not surprising we are human rather than chimpanzee or dolphin.

Chapter 6

Evolution, the heart of creativity

> The principle of generating small amounts of finite improbability by simply hooking the logic circuits of a Bambleweeny 57 Sub-Meson Brain to an atomic vector plotter suspended in a strong Brownian Motion producer (say a nice hot cup of tea) were of course well understood — and such generators were often used to break the ice at parties by making all the molecules in the hostess's undergarments leap simultaneously one foot to the left, in accordance with the Theory of Indeterminacy.
>
> *Douglas Adams*

About 150 years ago, Charles Darwin's *Origin of the Species* was published, introducing an idea so profound, and so controversial that it has ferocious condemnation from some, and ecstatic allegiance, bordering on religious zealotry from others. It has been misused to support appalling social and political doctrines. Daniel Dennett sums up this effect with *Darwin's Dangerous Idea*[42].

Evolution originally meant any process of change. The fossil record demonstrates that the species existing now are quite different to the species existing millions of years in the past. Numerous examples of species' form changing into others is documented in the fossil record. This "evolution of the species" rocked the world in the 19th century, which largely viewed the world as young, a few thousand years at most, and immutable. A few thousand years is insufficient time for Darwin's process of random accumulation of adaptions, and even when the Earth's age was estimated to be of the order of 100 million years in 1862 by Lord Kelvin, there didn't seem to be sufficient time for evolution to produce the rich tapestry of life we see today. However, Lord Kelvin didn't know about radioactivity, which was discovered in the closing years of the 19th century. Radioactive dating of rocks in the 20 century finally confirmed the age of the Earth at around 4550 million years old, considered a sufficiently ancient time for evolution to have worked its miracle.

Darwin's theory explaining the change as one of *variation* of individual phenotypes, upon which *natural selection* acts was so pivotal to the acceptance of changing species, that the term *evolution* now refers to this process of variation and selection.

We want to consider evolution more generally. Not only do species evolve, but so do cultures, languages and technology. New cultural elements arise as someone decides to do some particular act for whatever reason. If that idea has characteristics that make other people adopt it, then we can say the idea has *replicated*, or reproduced itself in another person's mind. Richard Dawkins introduced the concept of *meme*[36] to represent the notion of these ideas replicating and evolving in time, the cultural evolution equivalent to *gene*. Meme itself is a meme, and has taken on a life of its own, and has its own field of study: *mimetics*.

Languages and technology can be seen to be special cases of mimetic evolution. In the case of languages, words are labels for concepts (which are memes too, undergoing their own evolution). Words undergo evolution, as does the language grammar. As different population groups form, and mix with other population groups, different selection effects predominate. Sometimes selection favours the formation of new words, with the new words deployed as a kind of "membership badge" for the group using it. At other times, the need to communicate will have a harmonising effect on language, with common words displacing less common alternatives, and simplification of grammar. Professional communities will often need to make up new words to represent compound concepts more compactly, aiding communication.

Technology is a clear example of an evolutionary process. Obviously technical superiority of a good is a selection factor, but many other factors are important, including economics (inferior, but cheaper goods may be "fitter"), marketing and fashion (fashionable goods have an enormous selection advantage, albeit only for a limited period of time).

Beyond the areas of culture, and affiliated processes such as language and technology, evolution can also be seen in other processes. Popper describes science as a process of falsification. Scientific theories must be *falsifiable*. There must be tests of the theories such that the outcomes of those tests could prove the theory *wrong*. Of course if a scientific theory passes many such tests, then our belief in such a theory increases, however we can never know if a scientific theory is correct — there may be another test around the corner which the theory fails. There may be another theory (and usually there are several) that also pass the same battery of tests. We can never know if a theory is true, but can know ones that are false. A theory which cannot be be falsified is *unscientific*. An example of such a theory is notion of the world being created by an omnipotent being a few thousand years ago. The fact that evidence from radioactive isotopes implies the world is thousands of millions of years old can be explained away by having the Creator arranging the radioactive isotopes in such a way as to give the appearance of a world millions of times older than it. Of course why a Creator might do this defies logical reason. This does not falsify the theory — a situation summarised neatly by the epithet *God moves in mysterious ways.*

Scientific progress happens through new theories being proposed, and then tested via experimentation. False theories are typically discarded, theories which survive many such tests are "fit" in a Darwinian sense, and will be used for a long time.

Interestingly, falsified theories aren't always discarded. An example is Newton's theory of gravitational attraction, which does not correctly predict the orbit of Mercury. Einstein's theory of *General Relativity* does correctly predict Mercury's orbit, so it might seem that Newton's theory should be discarded for Einstein's. However, calculating the consequences of Einstein's field equations requires the esoteric branch of mathematics known as *tensor calculus*, which is algorithmically more complex than the computations used in Newton's theory. Newton's theory is sufficiently accurate that NASA can plot the trajectories of its interplanetary spacecraft using it, and its computational simplicity relative to Einstein's theory ensures its survival as a useful or "fit" theory.

6.1 Evolution in the Multiverse

Richard Lewontin categorises evolution as a process that satisfies the following 3 principles[80]:

1. *Variation* of individuals making up the population.

2. *Differential reproduction and survival* leading to natural *selection*.

3. *Heritability* of characteristics between parents and offspring.

The 3rd criterion, which is often not appreciated, is essential to prevent information created by selection from leaking away according to the second law of thermodynamics.

Let us now consider how evolution looks in a Multiverse bird perspective. In this perspective, no species ever becomes extinct. There will always be branches of the multiverse in which any phenotypic trait survives. We must replace differential survival with differential changes in measure for each trait. Only in the frog perspective do traits die out and become selected. Natural selection is actually anthropic selection (§5.3)[124].

Consider now an arbitrary physical process occurring in the Multiverse. The Multiverse itself is deterministic and time reversible. It is possible to compute the future history of the Multiverse's state knowing its present state, and it's possible to compute its past history as well, using an equation known as Schrödinger's equation. However, an observer in the frog perspective will continually make measurements of the Multiverse's state, restricting er experience to an ever diminishing slice of the Multiverse. In the frog perspective, what is observed is a nondeterministic, irreversible process. The equations describing the time evolution of the Multiverse, describe how the Multiverse *differentiates* into many different parallel worlds. This is Lewontin's first principle, that of *variation*. Anthropic selection takes the place of natural selection. Finally, the Schrödinger equation states that the state vector evolves *continuously* in time, implying that successor states of the Multiverse tend to be similar to their predecessor states. This last property matches the final *heritability* principle of Lewontin. Physics, as seen from the frog perspective, is an outcome of an evolutionary process.

When I first publicly discussed this idea in a lecture in 1998, a member of the audience immediately raised Lee Smolin's idea[121] of applying evolution to the universe as a whole, mentioned previously on page 49.

Smolin's scenario has all the hallmarks of an evolutionary process — variation, heredity and selection via anthropic selection. The view that I'm putting forward is that all irreversible physical processes are in fact evolutionary in nature. In chapter 7, we shall apply this idea to measurement, and end up with the structure of quantum mechanics.

6.2   Creativity

Many evolutionary processes are creative. There are more species alive now than at any other time in Earth's history. The well known paleobiologist Michael Benton[15] goes as far as saying that life's diversity has increased exponentially, a veritable explosion of form and function, at least for the last 600 million years for which we have a good fossil record. Evolution of life on earth is a tremendously creative process, seemingly without limit.

We are currently living in a time of tremendous technological revolution. New ideas and inventions appear each year, which in turn feed into next year's ideas and inventions. Vastly more science has been explored in the last century than in the previous millennia of human history. There appears to be no limits to how much knowledge we're capable of uncovering.[1]

These creative processes are evolutionary, what other creative processes might there be? Two that immediately come to mind is the creativity of the human mind, and the creativity inherent in the Cosmos. In a Multiverse setting, we have already seen the universe's structure created via an evolutionary process. I would like to suggest that consciousness too is an evolutionary process.

The nature of human creativity, and of consciousness, is the holy grail of science. A branch of computer science, *artificial intelligence*, concerns itself with the task of creating conscious machines. This quest was proposed by Alan Turing shortly after the first electronic computers were developed. Since then we have become very good at designing machines that can solve problems such as playing logical games like chess, solving some real world problems such as navigating a simple natural environment, and in the last couple of years, tremendous progress has been achieved in controlling a robotic body with legs — something animals have done with ease for millions of years. However, we cannot yet make a creative machine, after some 50 years of trying! A two year old child will outperform any computer program in terms of ideas generated and explored. As for making a conscious machine, the quest seems more hopeless than ever. The debate as

---

[1] Although recently Jonathon Huebner[68, 4] has claimed that the per capita innovation rate peaked a century ago, and has been falling ever since. Absolute innovation is at an all time high, however, due to the all time high population levels.

to what consciousness is is a quagmire[16, 41, 26], with seemingly more different ideas as to what it all means than there are researchers in the field.

Why might I be suggesting evolutionary processes as the key to consciousness? The most obvious is that evolution is the only creative mechanical process known to us, yet this is a little lame and unconvincing. Just because these are the only processes we know about doesn't rule out consciousness as being potentially a completely different kind of process. However, there is more evidence. Brains are the physical correlate of the mind, and we do know something of brains from neurophysiology. The first is that it is a network of cells, called neurons, that propagate electrical impulses down long fibres called *axons*. A neuron receives a number of electrical inputs from a number of neurons, sums the results, and if greater than a certain threshold, fires an electrical spike down its axon. The signals pass across a *synaptic gap* between the end of the axon and the next cell.

Artificial neural networks (ANNs) abstract the complexity of individual biological neurons, and replace them with simple functions of the sums of the inputs. The artificial neurons are wired up, either fully, or in some hierarchical scheme, and the weights on all the connections are adjusted via a learning algorithm to train the ANN. ANNs have been successfully deployed on a variety of artificial intelligence tasks, such as vision recognition and robot control. The simplest model of what an ANN does, is that of *content addressable memory*. It consists of a many-to-one map between data and a finite range of output responses. The map is robust to noise, in that small deviations in the input data will not tend to affect the final output. In content addressable memory, a small part of the data (eg the first line of a song) is sufficient to retrieve the full item of data. This, of course, sounds just like the observer map described in the discussion of the White Rabbit problem on page 61. This is not a coincidence — I was aware of this property of ANNs prior to postulating the robustness property as a solution to the White Rabbit problem.

Another view of the operation of an ANN is the dynamic one. *Dynamical Systems* is a branch of mathematics dealing with systems that change over time according to nonlinear equations of motion. The planets of the Solar System moving under Newton's law of gravitation is just such an example. For certain values of system parameters, the motions become unpredictable, a state called *deterministic chaos*. Dynamical Systems is often called *Chaos Theory* as a result. Dynamical Systems supplies the important concept of an *attractor*, which is a set of points to which the system converges. The set of initial conditions for which the system converges to a given attractor is called its *basin of attraction*. Attractors are classified as a point attractor (stable equilibrium), a limit cycle (periodic behaviour) or a *strange attractor* (chaotic behaviour). Artificial neural networks are high dimensional dynamical systems, but when used as content addressable memories, the dynamics is described as a set of point attractors. The output of the ANN will converge to the attractor whose basin of attraction contains the input (eg a song will have its first line contained with its basin of attraction).

So at the physiological level, brains are structured somewhat like artificial neural networks, which in turn act like filters, filtering a range of inputs down to a small finite set of outputs. This is thought to be a fairly good description of brains of very simple creatures, such as the *C. Elegans* nematode worm. However, brains of more complex creatures would be expected to be more than a very complex ANN. If we think of the brain as operating as an evolutionary process, then the biological neural network provides the selection mechanism — filtering out those combinations of inputs that aren't useful to the organism. To have evolution, we also must have a source of variation. Within the brain, this is most likely to lie in the synapse, which transmits the signal chemically across the synaptic gap. Being chemical in nature, there are small fluctuations in the time it takes for the signal to cross the gap. Depending on the dynamical nature of the neural network, the affect of these natural variations are either damped, or amplified. If the neural network dynamics is damped, we would expect to see only short range correlations in the time series recorded from an electro-encephalograph (EEG). If on the other hand, the brain was amplifying the inherent randomness across the synaptic junction, we would expect to see long range correlations in the EEG time series, ie the hallmarks of *Chaos*. A chaotic brain would be harnessing the butterfly effect to amplify natural synaptic randomness, thus providing the necessary variation for an evolutionary process.

Does the brain exhibit chaotic behaviour? People only really started looking at this question a decade or so ago, and there isn't really a consensus on the issue. Walter Freeman, an early pioneer of this field has concluded that chaos "may be the chief property that makes the brain different from an artificial-intelligence machine"[51].

6.3   Creating the creative machine

One would think from the above discussion that evolutionary processes are the key to creativity. A branch of computer science has developed called *evolutionary algorithms*, which apply Darwin's idea in a computer program to solving computer science problems. Getting robots to walk has only been achieved by evolving the algorithms according to a fitness measure of how well the robots walked. Computer scientist John Koza has created several patents in electronic circuits via a technique called evolutionary programming. This illustrates that creativity is possible in a purely mechanical process. Yet this creativity is strictly bounded. Usually, in an evolutionary algorithm, once an optimal solution to the problem is found, all evolution stops. Great care must be taken in choosing the representation of the problem, and what constraints are placed on the evolutionary search. Without constraints, the search space is too large and typically the evolutionary algorithm flounders around not finding anything at all. This is a long way from the ideal of an automatic creation machine — one that continuously generates new ideas as the human brain appears to be capable of.

So is it possible to produce an unboundedly creative machine? Scientists generally assume that a human being is such a machine, one created by the blind forces of natural evolution. This is a working hypothesis as nobody has proved human beings are machines. Nevertheless, to assume otherwise, to assume that we are animated by some kind of *vitalistic force*, or *soul* that is beyond the ken of human science would be to give up this quest entirely. The mechanistic nature of human beings is a faith, capable of receiving support when such a creative machine is unambiguously created through our technological efforts, but not capable of falsification. Lack of success in this quest can simply mean that we have not been clever enough!

At the Artificial Life 7 conference held in Portland, Oregon, in 2000, I had the pleasure to partake in a round-table discussion to thrash out the big open problems in the field of artificial life. A list of 14 open problems was eventually selected, and a description published in the Artificial Life journal[13]. At the conference itself, the one question on everyone's lips was how to generate an open-ended artificial evolutionary system. This particular question fed into several of the more specific challenges reported in the above cited paper.

Part of the problem here is defining precisely what we mean by "open-ended" evolution, or "creative" evolution. What seems fairly clear is that we're not interested in processes that only produce new things, without the new things being somehow better. The attitude taken by most artificial life researchers, including myself, is that *complexity* is the most relevant quantity. By complexity, most people mean something like the complexity measure defined in eq. (2.1). In applying that measure we need to determine the relevant syntactic and semantic languages. Many artificial life systems, such as Tom Ray's Tierra[109], or Chris Adami's Avida[1] already have an explicit syntactic language, the language of the artificial organism's *genome*. The semantic languages is often specified by whatever characterises the organism's phenotype. Chris Adami was one of earliest researchers to apply this form of complexity to an artificial life system, Avida. Avidan organisms do not interact with other, but do interact with an environment in the form of logical tasks, which if successfully achieved by the organism increases the organism's evolutionary fitness. The phenotype of such organisms is particularly easy to define in this case. Adami, and his coworkers, demonstrated periods of limited complexity growth, by manually changing the "goal posts" of the environmental task[1, 3]. However, by no stretch of the imagination was open-ended evolution demonstrated. I applied Adami's techniques to Tierra, which is a more difficult system to analyse since the organisms interact with each other[126]. I have achieved some limited increase in complexity over the ancestral organism[127], but no startling increases in complexity corresponding to Benton's exponential increase in biosphere diversity.

Mark Bedau has been vigorously promoting a *litmus test* of open-ended evolution[14]. He uses *diversity*, or number of different species of organism, as a proxy for complexity. Diversity is not enough, however, as a completely random process can generate arbitrary amounts of diversity. We also need to have some measure of how much *adaption* is going on in the evolutionary system. He, and his colleague Norm Packard, have defined two new measures for arbitrary evolutionary processes both natural and artificial, which they call the *extent* and *intensity* of the evolutionary process. Bedau and his coworkers have applied these measures to many different systems, and can classify evolutionary processes into four different classes. Not one artificial evolutionary system exhibits the same characteristics as the biosphere (so called *class 4* behaviour), yet he has seen some tentative evidence that technological evolution exhibits class 4 behaviour, using the US Patent Office database as a "fossil record" of technology[119].

Diversity is a proxy of the overall ecosystem complexity, not of its individual components. Whilst the increasing diversity pattern is clear in the biosphere as a whole, there are not so obvious trends in the complexity of individual organisms[98], aside from a few brief moments in evolutionary history, such as the Cambrian explosion[79]. In 1995, John Maynard Smith and Eörs Szathmáry proposed a sequence of major evolutionary transitions through which life on Earth passed[120], most involving a significant jump in organismal complexity. Several of these transitions, including the fusion of prokaryotic cells to form the eukaryotic cell,[2] and the evolution of multicellularity involve the synthesis of ecosystems into a new individual entity. Indeed, the human body (one of the most complex things in the universe) could quite rightly be considered as a very closely coupled ecosystem, not only of the human cells making up the body, but also of the microscopic flora and fauna inhabiting our guts, without which we could not survive, and which outnumber our own cells by a factor of 10[30].

It is clear, then, that we should be attempting to measure the complexity of emergent parts of the ecosystem that might correspond to new identities, rather than continuing to measure the complexity of individual organisms. However, this raises new open questions as to how to measure complexities of networks of entities, and of how to recognise emergent entities within an evolving ecosystem.

If a human being is a machine, then nature has already solved the problem of creating a creative machine. We must turn to nature for inspiration of how to solve this problem. Part of this question revolves around what

---

[2]Eukaryotic cells have a nucleus containing the bulk of the genetic material, and several specialised organelles, including the mitochondria, which have their own genetic material. All multicellular life forms, including animals, plants and fungi are based on eukaryotic cells. Prokaryotic cells on the other hand are simpler free living cells known as bacteria, and archeobacteria. Lynn Margulis proposed the *endosymbiotic theory* that claims eukaryotes arose through a symbiotic union of prokaryotic cells around a thousand million years ago.

we mean by machine. To a computer scientist, a machine means one thing — a device, or abstract object that can be exactly modelled by a *Turing Machine*. As mentioned previously, a universal Turing machine is a theoretical model of a computer, which can be made to emulate any other Turing machine by means of a suitable program. So the question can be recast as "does there exist a suitable program that makes my reference universal Turing machine U creative". From our discussion in chapter 3, if the observer knows the program, or can readily reverse engineer it, then the complexity of its output is bounded by the length of that program. So the creativity of this machine is strictly bounded. However, if the program were not so readily reverse-engineered, ie *cryptic* then the observed complexity of its output may well be unbounded.

Do such cryptic algorithms exist? We believe so. The RSA public key encryption algorithm is based on the belief that factoring a number into its primes factors is computationally infeasible if the factors are big enough. Here the precise meaning of these terms is the subject of a discipline called *Computational Complexity* (which differs from the *Algorithmic Complexity* theory we have referred to before). It hasn't been proven that there isn't a computationally efficient algorithm for factoring numbers, as this depends on proving an infamous conjecture known simply as $P \neq NP$, however computer scientists are sufficiently confident of its impossibility that banks regularly use the technology for securing large amounts of money. So an algorithm that depends in a fundamental way on multiplying two large prime numbers together cannot be reverse engineered, and so if not known by the observer will remain cryptic to an observer. Potentially, such an algorithm might display unbounded creativity.

The natural world has an advantage over the algorithmic in that genuine randomness is available through quantum processes. It is widely believed that the breakdown of atomic nuclei via beta decay is a completely random process. We may know on average that half of the atoms in a sample will decay within a time known as the *half life*, but we cannot predict which atoms will decay, nor when the decay events will occur. Can this randomness be exploited to generate unbounded creative processes? I have conducted some experiments using the Tierra system, where I have replaced the inbuilt random number generator with a source of real random numbers, and also with a presumed cryptic random generator algorithm. The results are still rather tentative, owing to computational difficulty in calculating complexities, but no real difference between the three sets of random number generators is observed.

Coupling such a source of true randomness to a computer is called using a *random oracle*. One of the earliest studies of random oracles proved that such a machine could not compute anything other than standard computable functions[37], however it is clear that such things may compute uncomputable things with certainty. Also, such machines tend to be more powerful at solving NP hard problems[27].

There is one way the quantum Multiverse can be used to generate complexity with assurity — couple the requirement of complexity with the anthropic principle. If observers are part of the system, and need a certain level of complexity in order to exist, then they will by necessity observe a system with growing complexity, much as we observe in the Biosphere. In effect, this is a type of quantum computing algorithm.

Possibly, quantum computers may be able to be harnessed to generate unboundedly creative systems, if the observers are co-evolved in the quantum system, and a suitable means of search (eg Grover's algorithm) could return the details of the creative branch[124].

6.4 Evolution as the Simplest Complexity Generator

The strong conclusion of this chapter is that evolutionary processes are the only mechanical processes capable of generating complexity. In the Multiverse, we saw that *all* irreversible processes were evolutionary in nature,[3] so this is somewhat of a truism.

The corollary of this point is that the simplest method of generating sufficient complexity in the universe to host a conscious observer is via an evolutionary process. Not only is life an evolutionary process, but physics is too. This requirement leads us to conclude that observer will almost certainly find themselves embedded in a Multiverse structure (providing the variation), observing possibilities turning into actuality (anthropic selection) inheritance of generated information (a form of differential or difference equation that preserves information, depending on the precise topology of time).

We shall see in the next chapter that this principle can be used to derive the fundamental postulates of quantum mechanics, showing that quantum mechanics is *the* theory of observation with continuous time.

---

[3]Reversible processes must conserve information, by definition

Chapter 7

Quantum Mechanics

> I think I can safely say that nobody understands Quantum Mechanics
>
> *Richard Feynman*

Richard Feynman was one of the geniuses of the 20th century[48]. He is perhaps most famously known for the *Feynman Lectures in Physics*, one of the most lucid treatments of modern physics, and an influential text for a generation of physicists. In the arena of quantum mechanics, he developed the formulation known as the *Path Integral Formulation* in the 1940s, which has proved an invaluable technique for evaluating quantum field theory (See [117] for an introduction). Feynman diagrams provide a graphical means of simplifying the computation of quantum field theory path integrals — recently, Feynman's "doodles" were celebrated on US postage stamps[148]. So when Feynman says he doesn't understand quantum mechanics, he doesn't mean that he doesn't understand the mathematics, nor that he doesn't understand the physical consequences of the theory. He means *understand* in the same manner that David Deutsch talks about understanding as explaining[43], not the "shut up and calculate" approach of *instrumentalism*. He means that he doesn't understand why the theory should have this particular form. Intuitively, it doesn't make sense. Yet the theory has been spectacularly confirmed by experiment, for example with the prediction of the spin magnetic moment for the electron which agrees with experiment to 10 decimal places[108].

The explanation of quantum mechanics as describing the process of observation within a plenitude of possibilities is for me the pinnacle of achievement of the paradigm discussed in this book. I can now say that I *understand* quantum mechanics. I want to share that understanding with you, the reader. I won't teach you the mathematical mechanics of quantum mechanics, which you will need if you wish to apply the theory — there are many of those sorts of books already. However, I will show you how to go from the elements I have already presented in this book to deriving the basic postulates of quantum mechanics, which are[117]:

1. There is a *state* of the system, which is represented by a vector ψ in a *Hilbert* space V.

2. The state vector ψ evolves in time according to the *Schrödinger equation*

$$i\hbar \frac{d\psi}{dt} = H\psi \qquad (7.1)$$

where H is a *Hermitian* linear operator on V called the *Hamiltonian*.

3. An observable is a Hermitian linear operator A, and the result on any measurement of the system is value that is one of the *eigenvalues* a of A, with

probability given by the formula (Born's rule):

$$P(a) = \frac{|\psi \cdot e_a|^2}{\psi \cdot \psi e_a \cdot e_a} \qquad (7.2)$$

4. For every system described in classical mechanics by a classical Hamiltonian (a function of position and momenta of all the constituent particles), the quantum Hamiltonian H is obtained by substituting the position variable x with the multiplication operator X ($X\psi(x) = x\psi(x)$), and the momentum variable p by the derivative operator $P = -i\hbar\frac{d}{dx}$. This is called the *correspondence principle*.

Phew! No wonder nobody understands quantum mechanics you might say. Actually the mathematical ideas above are not too hard to understand, once I tell you what they mean. The first idea is that of a *vector*, which is introduced in more detail in Appendix A. A vector is a mathematical object that has both a magnitude and a direction. A Hilbert space is a vector space having an inner product. The usual three dimensional space of our experience is a Hilbert space, so is the space of quantum states.

Observables correspond to Hermitian operators — these are linear functions, or operators, whose eigenvalues are real valued. Again these concepts are introduced in Appendix A.

If you have struggled with the above concepts, it is probably because you are wondering what this has to do with the physical world. You are not alone in this. If these concepts are unfamiliar to you, it is probably because you haven't studied science or engineering at university level, as students of these courses will typically come across these concepts in first year. If you consider the above as pure mathematical objects, and just

"shut up and calculate", it is not difficult to calculate
with them.

7.1   Deriving the Postulates

I have already published a detailed mathematical derivation of the quantum mechanical postulates elsewhere[128],
so instead of the gory detail, I would like to flesh out the
argument verbally. I provide the mathematical detail in
appendix D. It is modified slightly from the presentation
[128] to integrate it better into this book.

The first move I'd like to make is give an interpretation to the magnitude of the ψ vector. In standard
quantum mechanics, only the directional component of ψ
has physical significance, multiplying ψ by an arbitrary
complex number $A \in \mathbb{C}$ does not change the probabilities
given by the Born rule (7.2). In §4.4, I introduce the concept of observer moment to refer to the knowledge state
of an observer at a point in time. The state vector ψ
corresponds to this observer moment. Each observer moment has a measure, corresponding in loose terms to the
number of observers experiencing that observer moment.
Loose terms indeed, as I argue in §4.5 that measure can
be complex. In appendix C I show how it is possible to
determine for some complex measures which observer moments are likely to be selected under the self sampling assumption. Complex numbers are the most general mathematical field, and it would appear that the measure from
which observer moments are are drawn needs to be field
valued.

In chapter 6, I argued that physics itself must be
evolutionary, that evolutionary systems are the simplest
means of generating sufficient complexity to host an observer. We need to apply Lewontin's principles, the first

being that of *variation*. Remember that ψ is a dual concept, with the dual of state being the set of possible descriptions compatible with that state. There is a choice in how an observer will discriminate this set of possibilities — for example one may choose whether to measure the position of some particle, or its momentum. Once a choice of measurement has been made though, it partitions ψ in a set of discrete possibilities, $\psi_a, a = 0, 1, \ldots$.

Lewontin's second principle is that of selection, for which we take anthropic selection. Each of the ψ_a is selected with a certain probability $P_\psi(\psi_a)$, to be determined later. The combination of these two principles, multiverse variation and anthropic selection I call the PROJECTION postulate.

Linearity of the set of states turns out to come from additivity property of measure (4.1), when considering sets of observers drawn from a complex measure as part of the system. It is a somewhat technical argument, to which I refer the interested reader to appendix D.

With the property of linearity established, it turns out to be easy to relate the probabilities of observed outcomes to projections of the system's state onto the new state, and to show that this projection is in the form of an inner product (7.2).

Finally, we have Lewontin's third principle, heritability of acquired characteristics. Between observer moments, information must be preserved. After mapping the ordered sequence of observer moments into the real number line, this implies a differential evolution equation mapping the ψ_a selected at one observer moment to the ψ ensemble appearing at the next observer moment.

Linearity of this differential equation follows from the requirement that linear combinations of states must also be solutions of this equation, and the Hermitian property follows from conservation of probability across the Multiverse, ie *in the Multiverse, something always happens.*

This takes care of the first three postulates — I have left the fourth postulate for last because, it is rather different to the other three. It is basically in the form of a principle that can generate a specific form of the Schrödinger equation, based on the classical mechanical description of the system. Also, as a principle it is rather unsatisfactory, as the P and X operators do not commute, ie $PX \neq XP$. So one can generate different quantum Hamiltonians from the same classical Hamiltonian, if the classical Hamiltonian has x and p multiplied together. There are also quantum systems (eg particles with spin) that simply have no classical counterpart, so the fourth postulate cannot be applied. Which really tells us that the correspondence principle is not much more than a "rule of thumb", and that deducing the real quantum Hamiltonian is a form of black art, backed up with guidance from experiment.

So when I say I understand quantum mechanics, I mean that I know that the first three postulates are directly consequences of us being observers. Quantum mechanics is simply a theory of observation! Might the correspondence principle, however, provide a way for the noumenon to exert its influence? Is it a possible link to things as they really are, rather than how we observe them?

7.2   The Correspondence Principle explained

The heart of the correspondence principle is the identification of the multiplication operator $X\psi(x) = x\psi(x)$ with position and the derivative operator $P\psi(x) = -i\hbar\frac{d\psi(x)}{dx}$

with momentum. Victor Stenger has a very good explanation for why this is so, based on the concept of *gauge invariance*[130]. It is not germane to the present discussion to reproduce mathematical detail well covered elsewhere, so I recommend the interested reader to the detailed mathematical treatment in appendix D of Stenger's book.

Consider a single point particle in a four dimensional space-time. It has four coordinates representing where the particles are in space, and when in time. Since the particle has no other properties other than where and when it is, we can write its state as a function of its coordinates $\psi(t, x, y, z)$. The *laws of physics* describing the particle cannot depend on how you define the origin of your coordinate axes, nor on how you orient the axes, so are *gauge invariant*. In particular, the distance between two points in our coordinate space cannot depend on the choice of origin or orientation of our axes. The derivative is the limit of a difference between two points, divided by the distance between them, so it too is gauge invariant. Gauge invariance is not a *physical* principle, but a *logical* principle. To deny its applicability would be to assert that there is some preferred coordinate system, for which we have no evidence. Heed Occam's razor: preferred coordinate systems add an extra level of unneeded complexity, thus should be discarded as an unnecessary hypothesis. What is left is gauge invariance.

In the *Special Theory of Relativity*, spacetime has what is called a Minkowskian structure. To explain what this is, consider Pythagoras's theorem for right angle triangles, namely that the square of the hypotenuse is the sum of the squares of the other two sides. Mathematically, it has the form $a = \sqrt{b^2 + c^2}$. Embedding our triangle into three dimensions gives us a formula for the distance between two points (x_1, y_1, z_1) and (x_2, y_2, z_2):

$$d = \sqrt{(x_1 - x_2)^2 + (y_1 - y_2)^2 + (z_1 - z_2)^2}$$

Extending this formula to four dimensions seems trivial, all we'd need to do is add an extra term $c^2(t_1 - t_2)^2$ inside the square root above, c being a conversion factor relating spatial units to time units (eg in metres per second). Spaces obeying a distance rule (called a metric) like this are called *Euclidean*, after the famous ancient Greek geometer who formalised geometry. However, it turns out that the space-time we live in does not behave in a Euclidean fashion, and we should in fact subtract the time term:

$$d = \sqrt{c^2(t_1 - t_2)^2 - (x_1 - x_2)^2 - (y_1 - y_2)^2 - (z_1 - z_2)^2}$$
$$(7.3)$$

Spaces with a metric like Eq. (7.3) are called *Minkowskian*. This distance is a positive real number for any two events linked by something travelling less than the speed c (the "speed of light"). We call this the object's *proper time*. For events widely separated in space, the term inside the square root is negative, so the distance d is imaginary. In this case, no unique ordering of events in time is possible. Causal influences travelling faster than c lead to temporal paradoxes. For particles travelling at the speed of light, $d = 0$ for all events it passes though. For such a particle, the universe's entire history vanishes in the blink of an eye. All of relativity's well-known nonintuitive results can all be explained in terms of the single equation (7.3).

The 4-vector $\nabla \psi \equiv (\frac{\partial \psi}{\partial t}, \frac{\partial \psi}{\partial x}, \frac{\partial \psi}{\partial y}, \frac{\partial \psi}{\partial z})$ is gauge invariant, and so is a 4-vector made up of the eigenvalues of these operators. The length of this 4-vector is an intrinsic property of the particle, independent of the velocity and location of the observer. For an ideal, electrically neutral, point particle, the only intrinsic property of the particle is its mass m. Since mass has not yet been defined in quantum mechanics, we are free to identify the length of the eigenvalues of ∇ with mass. By virtue of the Minkowskian structure, the projection of this 4-vector onto three dimensional space is the particle's momentum, and the projection onto the time axis is its energy. At low velocities compared with the speed of light, momentum is approximately $\vec{p} \approx m\vec{v}$, and energy is approximately $E \approx mc^2 + \frac{1}{2}mv^2$, which readers will recognise as the classical formulae for these terms.

Victor Stenger has effectively moved the mystery of the correspondence principle into the mystery of why we find ourselves in a 4D Minkowskian space-time. However, the argument would work regardless of what dimensionality our space time is. We'll come back to this point in a later section.

7.3 The principle of Extreme Physical Information

You may be starting to feel a little uncomfortable in the notion that the mysterious quantum mechanics is nothing more than a consequence of how we observe things. Perhaps you think that I'm doing some fancy mathematical footwork. You will be interested that my derivation is not the only one starting from considering the process of observation. Roy Frieden has developed another approach, which he calls *Extreme Physical Information*.

The Fisher information measure

$$I = \int (p'(x))^2 / p(x) dx \qquad (7.4)$$

provides a measure for the error in estimating the mean

of the probability distribution $p(x)$ by sampling it repeatedly. The minimum possible mean-square error e^2 obeys the *Cramer-Rao* inequality:

$$e^2 I \geq 1 \qquad (7.5)$$

The formula for Fisher information needs to be modified to handle the sampling of vector valued quantities, but the exact details is not relevant here.

The idea here is that an ideal observer affects the system being observed, to the point of seeing a distribution that maximises I, and minimises the inherent error in the measurement process. The probability distribution $p(x)$ in equation (7.4) is found by a mathematical technique called *Calculus of Variations*. Classical calculus find the maximum (or minimum) of some function by finding the point where the slope (or derivative) equals zero. In calculus of variations, we find the maximum (or minimum) of a quantity that depends on a function (eg $p(x)$) rather than a single variable like x.

For any physical process, there are also constraints such as conservation of mass/energy/momenta (which is basically the gauge invariance we discussed in the last section) that also must be satisfied by the probability distribution $p(x)$. To include the effect of system constraints, a technique called *Lagrange multipliers* is used, which effectively adds a second component to the Fisher information. Frieden shows that this term has opposite sign to I, so writes the extremum principle[1] as optimising the *Kantian*, or physical information $K = I - J$. J he calls *bound information*, and contains all the relevant physical constraints for the measurement being considered.

The solution to an extremum problem is given by a partial differential equation called an *Euler-Lagrange*

---

[1] An extremum is either a maximum or a minimum

equation. This equation is part of a mathematical recipe called calculus of variations, a straight-forward mathematical derivation. For appropriately chosen constraints (gauge invariance etc.) various Euler-Lagrange equations can be derived, including the *Klein Gordon equation* (a relativistic version of Schrödinger's wave equation), *Maxwell's equations* of electromagnetism and *Einstein's field equation* from General Relativity.

In the *Principle of Extreme Physical Information* (EPI), Frieden has at a stroke discovered a way of basing the foundational cornerstones of 20th century physics on the properties of the observer (I) and the logical constraints in the choice of observable (J).

7.4 Marchal's theory of COMP

Bruno Marchal, a philosopher based in Brussels, is a long time contributer to the *Everything list*. He explores the consequences of the *computationalist* (§4.7) model of consciousness. We have already mentioned how the ability to copy a conscious mind necessarily introduces indeterminism into the first person experience of that consciousness. If we are computers, then we must live in a many worlds ensemble.

Since we are assuming computationalism, we can examine the structure of what we can know via application of logic, in particular *modal logic*[18]. Modal logic is particularly apt for describing many worlds situations. Over and above the usual operations and constants of classical logic ($\top$="true", $\bot$="false", $\wedge$ = "and", $\vee$ = "or", $\neg$ = "not", $\rightarrow \equiv a \vee \neg b$ = "entails" or "implies"), there are two new symbols $\square$ and $\diamond$. In a multiple worlds setting, $\square p$ can be read as p is true in every world, and $\diamond p$ reads as p is true in at least one world. $\square$ and $\diamond$ are always related to each other, you could consider $\Box$ as primitive, and $\Diamond = \neg\Box\neg$, or $\Diamond$ as primitive, and $\Box = \neg\Diamond\neg$. Of course modal logic is a purely formal subject, and one is free to choose the interpretations of the different symbols. From your chosen interpretation as a model, certain axioms (statements that are accepted as true without proof) become apparent, and using standard rules of inference, one can deduce theorems that follow from the axioms. If you have come across the existential qualifiers $\forall$ and $\exists$, you might notice that $\forall = \neg\exists\neg$ and $\exists = \neg\forall\neg$, so $\Box$ and $\Diamond$ are generalisations of these very familiar qualifiers.[2]

Boolos's book[18] is mainly about the logic of provability, the modal logic G[3] where $\Box p$ is interpreted as p can be *proven* using (eg) the Peano axioms of arithmetic. $\Diamond p = \neg\Box\neg p$ is then interpreted as p is *consistent* with the Peano axioms. For example, Gödel's famous second incompleteness theorem[65] can be written succinctly as:

$$\Diamond\top \rightarrow \neg\Box\Diamond\top \tag{7.6}$$

"Consistent arithmetic cannot prove its own consistency". Statement (7.6) is a theorem of G and can be proved in about 2 lines.

To a logician, provability is equivalent to believability. In mathematics, we only believe a statement is true if it can be deduced from the set of axioms that we believe a priori. This differs somewhat from the everyday use of belief, which might be closer to the meaning of consistent — I will believe what Fred just told me, because it is consistent with what I know, and I think Fred

---

[2]And once again, we have demonstrated that old logic joke, "$\forall\forall\exists\exists$" (which reads "for every upside down A, there is a back-to-front E")!

[3]Boolos changed his notation in [18] from G to GL (L for Löb), and from G^* to GLS. I will continue to use the older notation here, as this is what Marchal uses in his work.

is a trustworthy fellow. To a mathematician, however, that is not good enough. Fred needs to demonstrate by means of a formal proof that his statement is correct, in order to be believed. In order to clarify the relationship between different possible modal logics, in a later paper Marchal introduces the symbol B to stand for belief or provability[89]. So we read Bp as meaning that we believe p, and the modal system G corresponds to the identity $\Box \equiv B$. The complementary symbol is $D = \neg B \neg$.

Now it turns out that $Bp \to p$ is not a theorem of G (one cannot prove that provability of a statement entails its truth), so we construct another logic system G^* from G that asserts truth of provable statements. One of the rules of inference is no longer valid (the rule of necessitation or generalisation), so the logic must be seeded by all theorems of G as axioms (we don't concern ourselves with the fact that this is hardly a minimal set, nor necessarily reducible to a finite set of axioms), and then add $Bp \to p$ as another axiom. G and G^* are not identical, and the difference between the two, $G^* \backslash G$, is also a logic system, which Marchal identifies with *unbelievable truth*. As an example of this category, he refers to his parable of the brain transplant patient. The doctor performing the transplant can never prove to you that you will survive the operation (although this is true by assumption). After all, perhaps it is someone else who wakes up in your body with a copy of your mind.

The assumption that a concrete reality exists is superfluous with computationalism, Marchal then attempts to derive the appearance of physics from logical considerations of *knowledge*. The aim here is to attempt to drive a contradiction between predictions of computationalism, and empirical science. Of course, to date, the logic of knowledge is consistent with the theory of quantum mechanics.

Marchal identifies $Cp \equiv Bp \wedge p$ with "to know p" using Theaetetus's idea of knowledge, as related by Plato in his book *Theaetetus*, i.e. that we can know something if it is both true and can be proven. Identifying $\Box \equiv C$ gives rise to a logic known cryptically as S4Grz, and Marchal identifies this with the subjective world. There are no unknowable truths.

To describe physics, or the phenomenology of matter, we need to introduce consistency. Marchal considers two variants of the Theaetetus idea by adding consistency to belief and knowledge respectively:

$Pp \equiv Bp \wedge Dp$ To "bet" on p

$Op \equiv Cp \wedge Dp \wedge p$ To correctly "bet" on p

Bet is a somewhat of a strange verb here. The logic is the logic of probability 1, ie p true implies something happens with certainty. Perhaps "sure bet" is more precise, yet the language becomes cumbersome. Inconsistent knowledge can presumably be relegated to dreams.

Furthermore, we are also interested only in proofs that can be found in the output of the universal dovetailer. Technically, these statements are known as Σ_1, and the restriction of G and G^* to Σ_1 proofs is called V and V^* after Albert Visser. Applying the equivalences $\Box = B, P$ or O respectively to G, G^*, V and V^* leads to a total of 12 logic systems, as indicated in table 7.1, with only 10 distinct systems, as S4Grz=S4Grz* and S4Grz$_1$=S4Grz$_1^*$.

By a relatively complicated set of logical manipulations, Marchal shows that something called the Goldblatt transform applied to S4Grz$_1$, Z$_1$ and X$_1$ gives 3 different quantum logics, ie logics that describe the behaviour of vector subspaces, rather than of sets.[4]

---

[4]The intersection of two vector subspaces is a subspace, but the

	$\square \equiv B$	$\square \equiv C$	$\square \equiv P$	$\square \equiv O$
	G,G*	S4Grz,S4Grz	Z,Z*	X,X*
Σ_1 restriction	V,V*	S4Grz$_1$,S4Grz$_1$	Z$_1$,Z$_1^*$	X$_1$,X$_1^*$

Table 7.1: Marchal's menagerie of modal logics. The columns correspond to belief, knowledge, consistent belief and consistent knowledge. The Σ_1 restriction of consistent knowledge and belief are candidates for the phenomenology of matter

Thus Bruno has shown the "shadow" of the Hilbert space structure of quantum mechanics, from within a self-consistent theory of observerhood.[5] His conclusion is instead of psychology being reducible to, or indeed emerging from the laws of physics, the fundamental laws of physics are in fact a consequence of the properties of machine psychology. This is indeed a revolutionary *reversal* of the traditional ontology of these subjects. From my own approach described in §7.1, I agree with this fundamental tenant, but suspect that the TIME and PROJECTION postulates I start with may be more general than the computationalism hypothesis deployed by Marchal.

---

union is not, in general a subspace. If we interpret the $\vee$ operation as referring to the smallest vector subspace containing the union, then it is not hard to show that $A \wedge B \neq (A \wedge C) \vee (B \wedge \neg C)$ in general, whereas for sets $A \cap B = (A \cap C) \cup (B \cap \overline{C})$. The logic of statements of the form $a \equiv x \in A, b \equiv x \in B, \ldots$ when applied to sets gives the classical logic theorem $a \wedge b = (a \wedge c) \vee (a \wedge \neg c)$, which is false for quantum logics.

[5]These are his words, not mine. See [90] for an elaboration of these ideas in English.

7.5 Comparing the three "roads" to Quantum Mechanics

Each of the three approaches to quantum mechanics are somewhat complementary to each other, but share the consequence that quantum mechanics is a theory of observation. In my approach, the Plenitude is assumed, based on the arguments given in §3.2, and observers are assumed to obey the TIME and PROJECTION postulates. From this, and the mathematical properties of probability, we obtain the first three postulates of quantum mechanics, including linearity, unitarity and Born's rule (7.2). The fourth postulate (correspondence principle) can be obtained by considering gauge invariance. However, the precise form of the Schrödinger wave equation is not determined.

Frieden's approach on the other hand assumes linearity (Fisher information is the best linear unbiased estimate), unitarity (in order to create the precise form of J) and does not generate the probability formula — but does generate the Schrödinger wave equation (or at least its relativistic counterpart).

Finally Marchal's approach starts with assuming *computationalism*, and derives the existence of the Plenitude, and the linear structure of quantum mechanics. The advantage of Marchal's method is that it is more formal (hence stronger mathematically) than the other techniques, however its disadvantage is its reliance on computationalism, which is a controversial assumption. I also suspect that an appropriately formalised version of my TIME postulate can be derived from computationalism, so the methods are quite close.

7.6 Is an ensemble theory and a theory of consciousness the ultimate "Theory of Everything"?

Paraphrasing the title of Max Tegmark's paper, the fact that we can arrive at the theory of quantum mechanics within an ensemble theory, starting from three slightly different, but related, concepts of conscious experience, is heady stuff indeed. With the true hubris of a scientist, I would speculate we can do more. What about Einstein's theory of relativity, both the special and general form? As discussed in section §7.2, special relativity flows entirely from the Minkowskian structure of space time. The strange effects of temporal and mass dilation are simply the effects of different observers being at different orientations to each other within Minkowskian space-time.

General relativity follows from the observation that spacetime needn't be *flat*. Euclid's geometry, taught to generations of students, is an example of flat space. Triangles, for example have familiar properties in Euclidean spaces, such as the sum of the angles adding up to 180°, and Pythagoras's theorem holds for right angled triangles. However, of all of Euclid's axioms (assumptions), the fifth on the list proved most problematic. He assumes that two lines not parallel to each other will eventually intersect. For centuries, mathematicians tried to derive the fifth axiom from the others. It turns out that the fifth axiom is independent of the other axioms, and geometry is in fact more general than that captured by Euclid's axioms. A simple to understand example is the surface of a ball, such as the Earth. Imagine drawing an equilateral triangle with one vertex at the North Pole, and the other two vertices lying on the Equator. The three angles of the triangle are each 90°, so the sum of the angles is

270°. Also, you can clearly see that Pythagoras's theorem is false. In general no matter what size the triangle is drawn, the sum of the angles is always greater than 180°.

In general, spacetime is curved, and the curvature varies from point to point. Thus curved spacetimes should be preferred over flat one by application of Occam's Razor, which demurs arbitrary restrictions. Einstein's field equations links the amount of curvature to the distribution of mass-energy within spacetime. Understanding that curvature of spacetime should be related to mass in some way can be achieved by considering what mass means in the classical context.

In Newtonian physics, mass appears in the statement of Newton's second law as "inertial" mass:

$$F = ma \tag{7.7}$$

and also in the law of gravitation as gravitational mass:

$$F = \frac{GmM}{r^2} \tag{7.8}$$

Inertial mass and gravitational mass are assumed to be identical, and indeed this principle is canonized as the *equivalence principle* of General Relativity.

Combining equations (7.7) and (7.8) gives

$$a = \frac{GM}{r^2} \tag{7.9}$$

Curved spacetime will cause particle trajectories in free fall to diverge from the straight lines they will follow if spacetime were flat. This divergence will appear as an acceleration, which can be interpreted as a force. The curvature of spacetime will therefore appear to be due to a mass M gravitationally attracting the particle.

The exact form of the Einstein equations relating space-time curvature to mass distribution can be determined by Frieden's principle of extreme information.

In trying to extend our paradigm that consciousness determines the laws of physics, we need to establish reasons why we might find ourselves within (near-) Minkowskian spacetime, and why the generator of translation (the four dimensional derivative operator whose magnitude is mass) warps spacetime according to Einstein's equations.

This is all still an open question, but we can make some progress on the 3+1 spacetime dimensionality question. There are two somewhat speculative answers to this question, the first given by Max Tegmark[134]. He reviews evidence based on the mathematical form of equations describing gravity and/or electric force. The inverse square law of Newtonian gravity and Coulombic attraction between charged particles is actually rather special, in that it allows orbits in two body systems. No other force law has this property. Without stable orbits, one cannot have stable systems of finite size — they will either blow up, or shrink rapidly to a point.

Why might we think that the gravitational law would deviate from $\frac{1}{r^2}$ in higher or lower dimensional spaces than three? In three dimensions, an inverse square force is the derivative of a potential field that is a solution of *Poisson's equation* $\nabla^2 \phi = 0$. In a d-dimensional space with $d > 2$, Poisson's equation gives rise to a force law that is $\frac{1}{r^{d-1}}$. Poisson's equation is a particularly simple mathematical equation, and hints that even though inverse square forces may exist in higher dimensional spaces, they may be far more complex mathematically, hence at a lower measure in the ensemble of all descriptions.

Another possible answer to this question, which more

directly addresses why we don't appear in a 0,1 or 2D space, relates to topological effects on graphs. We assume that a self-aware observer is a complicated structure, a network of simpler components connected together. It is a well known result, that an arbitrary graph (or network) can be embedded into a 3 dimensional space, but two dimensional (or less) embedding spaces constrain the possible form of the graph. Connections between nodes (eg nerve fibres in the brain) cannot cross in a simple 2D space. Perhaps 2D spaces do not allow organisms to become sufficiently complex to become self-aware.

It is worth bearing in mind that the *Game of Life*[32] is a 2 dimensional cellular automata, that has been shown to be Turing complete. As a consequence, *computationalism* asserts that some pattern of cells with the Game of Life is, in fact, conscious. Nevertheless, the patterns in the Game of Life are very "brittle", and perhaps Darwinian evolution cannot function correctly in such a space. Perhaps it is the case that whilst self aware observers may be found within the Game of Life and other 2D universes, the overall measure of such observers is very low compared with 3 dimensional observers that have the advantage of evolving from simple initial conditions.

Having decided that space is most likely to be 3D, and time must be at least 1D, we need to ask the question of why these things appear in the Minkowski metric, with the time component having opposite sign in the metric to the spatial components. Tegmark here, gives a fascinating explanation based on the classification scheme of differential equations. Second order partial differential equations are classified according to the matrix of coefficients connecting the second order partial derivatives in the equation:

elliptic if all eigenvalues of the matrix have the same

sign

hyperbolic if one eigenvalue has the opposite sign of the rest

ultrahyperbolic if at least 2 eigenvalues are positive, and two negative

Interestingly, only hyperbolic equations lead to predictable physics, to a physical world that is computationally simple and likely to be observed. And with hyperbolic equations, the metric of the underlying space must have a Minkowski signature: $(+ - - - -)$, and if space is 3D, then time must be 1D.

Of course this begs the question of why second order partial differential equations should be so important in describing reality. Roy Frieden has the answer: the solution to the problem of finding the extremum of Fisher information is an *Euler-Lagrange* equation, which is always a 2nd order partial differential equation!

I'd like to end this chapter with a final observation that I'm very unsure of. Shun-ichi Amari has developed a theory of statistical estimation, as sort of Bayes' theorem on steroids that involves statistical models being updated as the result of new information. The passage of the statistical model through the hyperspace of the model's parameters turns out to be *geodesic* (a curve minimising distance between 2 points[6]) through a Riemannian space whose metric is given by Fisher information. The speculation I have is grafting this onto Roy Frieden's information demon and my TIME and PROJECTION postulates will generate a theory of Riemannian manifolds that includes our perceived spacetime, ie General Relativity. I'd like to think of this as a signpost — perhaps pointing to

---

[6]Such curves are lines in Euclidean spaces

the long desired grand unification of physics, but equally possibly pointing to a conceptual dead-end. Some brave intellectual will need to venture beyond the signpost to find out.

Chapter 8

Immortality

> Eternity is not something that begins after you're dead. It is going on all the time. We are in it now.
>
> *Charlotte Perkins Gilman*

In chapter 1, we saw how Schrödinger's cat developed a sense of invulnerability. No matter how long the experimenter continues the experiment, the cat never sees the radioactive atom decay, nor the vial of poison breaking. Similarly, when Tegmark stands in front of his quantum machine gun, he never sees the gun fire.

It is clear one can extend this argument to other forms of death. If one dies by a traffic accident, a heart attack or gunfire, there is clearly a random component to the outcome. If the dice rolls differently, death would be averted. There is some future of that moment in which one survives. By some version of the self-sampling assumption, this is what one would experience — we cannot experience our own annihilation.

What if this scenario were true of *all* causes of death? Then we must experience a sort of immortality. It is a first person immortal experience of course — other people will still see you die eventually of course.

The *Quantum Theory of Immortality* (QTI), is an idea whose time has come. Numerous times over the course of the Everything list's history, new people joining the list have suggested the idea, either based on considerations of Schrödinger's cat's experience, or on similar scenarios like Tegmark's suicide gun. James Higgo, an early Everything list contributer, whose life in this world was tragically prematurely ended in an aeroplane crash on July 22nd 2001[1] researched this theory extensively, and posted a lot of information on his website[61, 60]. It appears the earliest mention of the idea in print was Euan Squires book "The Mystery of the Quantum World"[123]. Don Page mentions that Edward Teller, "Father of the H bomb", first mentioned the immortality consequence in 1982, but Teller considered the prediction to be a form of *reductio ad absurdum* against the Many Worlds Interpretation[103].

8.1   Arguments against QTI

8.1.1   Maximum possible age

When people think of immortality, they usually think of eternal youth. The immortal gods of Greek and Roman legend are youthful, powerful and stay that way eternally. However, quantum immortality is not like that. You do experience aging, decrepitude and pain, without any hope of release from death. Its more of a sentence than a gift.

One possible objection against true immortality is

---

[1] All the more poignant in light of his discussion with Rainer Plaga about the possibility of Rainer's aeroplane crashing in November 1998[62]

that there might be some absolute logical reason why humans cannot live beyond a certain age. Insurance companies are, of course, keen to know if there are any fundamental limits to human longevity. During the 20th century, human lifetime expectancies have risen dramatically, leading some to predict life expectancies exceeding 100 years by the year 2060[71]. However, a more realistic appraisal of human biology indicates a "warranty period", during which genetic repair mechanisms are effective[25]. After the warranty expires, genetic errors accumulate rapidly, leading to age related disorders, and ultimately death.

However, it is true that people don't die of old age. Old people always die of a something, usually a disease whose likelihood increases dramatically with age. In all of these diseases, the actual time of death is randomly determined, the above argument still works and one expects to personally survive the illness (even if one's third person probability is extremely low).

Nevertheless, we have no experience of people living beyond the age of about 120. It is certainly conceivable that there is some absolute barrier preventing people aging beyond 200 (lets say). We don't know anyone who has lived that long to find out (save a few legendary figures mentioned in *Genesis*). We cannot rule out a hard maximum lifespan, but at this stage human life looks like being indefinitely extendible via medical intervention[74].

The possibility of an absolute maximum lifespan is a special case of a more general question — is there a physical situation one can get into from which death is certain, not merely likely, but certain. Such situations are termed *cul-de-sacs*, in the sense that once your consciousness enters such a state, there is no way out.

Are there any cul-de-sacs? Natural death doesn't

seem to offer any, however human ingenuity has been applied with great success to finding methods for killing people. The death penalty is applied in a number of countries, and in different times and places different methods were used to perform an execution. Obviously each method was refined to make death as likely as possible. The modern trend is also not to prolong the death, but make it as quick and painless as possible. Neither an efficient death, nor one that is uncertain leads to conscious states from which death is inescable. It is possible to survive the hangman's noose, for example, albeit with a broken neck. Also consciousness cannot resolve time more finely than a few 10ths of a second. If death is too rapid, then one couldn't possibly be conscious of any cul-de-sac moments prior to death.

Of all the execution methods used, decapitation appears to be the only method offering possible cul-de-sac conscious states. Certainly it seems difficult to imagine survival once the neck is severed. Does the condemned prisoner experience consciousness after decapitation? Medically, one would expect that consciousness would be lost rapidly once brain blood pressure dropped after the neck was severed, but to determine if conscious states do exist after decapitation requires performing the ultimate experiment. I'm not offering to do this myself, of course! However, the experiment has been done. Antoine Lavoisier was a famous chemist[2] living in France during the time of French revolution. At one point, he fell foul of the revolutionary committee, and was executed by means of the guillotine. An apocryphal story relates that he proposed to a colleague that he would perform this ultimate experiment by means of blinking his eye, so the colleague could determine how long consciousness might

---

[2]Famous for the discovery of Oxygen, amongst other things

last after decapitation. Reputedly Lavoisier's eye blinked for around 15 seconds after decapitation.[3] A better documented experiment concerns a man named Languille who was guillotined in 1905[72, page100]. A Dr Beaurieux, writing in *Archives d'Anthropologie Criminelle* states:

> "I waited for several seconds. The spasmodic movements ceased. The face relaxed, the lids half closed on the eyeballs, leaving only the white of the conjunctiva visible, exactly as in the dying whom we have occasion to see every day in the exercise of our profession, or as in those just dead. It was then that I called in a strong, sharp voice: "Languille!" I saw the eyelids slowly lift up, without any spasmodic contractions — I insist advisedly on this peculiarity — but with an even movement, quite distinct and normal, such as happens in everyday life, with people awakened or torn from their thoughts. Next Languille's eyes very definitely fixed themselves on mine and the pupils focused themselves. I was not, then, dealing with the sort of vague dull look without any expression, that can be observed any day in dying people to whom one speaks: I was dealing with undeniably living eyes which were looking at me. After several seconds, the eyelids closed again, slowly and evenly, and the head took on the same appearance as it had had before I called out.

---

[3]This story may be found in a number of sources on the internet, eg the Wikipedia entry for Lavoisier and the New Scientist "The last word" section from the 16th December 2000 issue. Each article stresses that none of the standard biographies mention this experiment, so it is probably nothing other than an urban myth.

> "It was at that point that I called out again
> and, once more, without any spasm, slowly,
> the eyelids lifted and undeniably living eyes
> fixed themselves on mine with perhaps even
> more penetration than the first time. Then
> there was a further closing of the eyelids, but
> now less complete. I attempted the effect of
> a third call; there was no further movement
> — and the eyes took on the glazed look which
> they have in the dead."

Taken at face value, this evidence points to plenty of cul-de-sac moments.

Of course, there are ways of getting around this scenario. Perhaps the beheaded experienced aliens landing on Earth at that moment, who resurrected him with advanced medical technologies. Perhaps a Victor Frankenstein actually existed who obtained Lavoisier's head, and attached his head to a "monster". Perhaps Lavoisier went to heaven and sat with angels. There are so many *possible* scenarios for what a decapitated head may experience afterwards, that it becomes completely impossible to say with certainty that these are cul-de-sac moments.

No matter how dire the situation, it is always possible to imagine a way of surviving, no matter how improbable. For a cul-de-sac moment, the probability of survival must be exactly zero. This leads to the *no cul-de-sac conjecture*, namely that there must always be some way of surviving every situation.

What evidence is there for the no cul-de-sac conjecture? How might it be proved? One means of formalising it is to use modal logic. In Kripke semantics, worlds are connected by means of an *accessibility* relation R. In terms of our picture of the Multiverse, worlds are observer moments and the accessibility relationship is that of successor observer moment. $\Box p$ is true in a world w, if p is true in all worlds accessed from w. $\Diamond p$ is true in a world w if p is true in at least one world accessible from w.

A world is called *terminal* if no worlds are accessible from it. These correspond to cul-de-sac observer moments. Clearly $\Box p$ is true for a terminal world, but not $\Diamond p$. So the deontic equation $\Box p \rightarrow \Diamond p$ can only be true in a logic that has no terminal worlds.

The TIME postulate can be formalised as an accessibility relationship between observer moments, considered as worlds. If the deontic relationship applies to all observer moments, then no cul-de-sac observer moments exist. Of all of Marchal's menagerie of logics (table 7.1) only G and V do not prove the deontic relation[91]. Of the logic systems giving quantum logics (S4Grz$_1$, Z$_1$ and X$_1$), only S4Grz$_1$ has a Kripke semantic, so at the present time, modal logic has not proven the no cul-de-sac conjecture.

8.1.2   Dementia

Of course, as one ages, dementia becomes increasingly likely. Perhaps eventually one's personal identity becomes so fractured by dementia that continued survival becomes impossible[133]. One possibility is that as memories fade, the conscious mind becomes similar enough to that of a new born baby, and one effectively experiences reincarnation. Why should we think that our conscious entity transfers "bodies" like that?

Bruno Marchal has demonstrated with computationalism that consciousness can not be aware of exactly which computation implements it. Instead, the consciousness supervenes on all identical computations implementing that consciousness[94]. Even under the more general as-

sumption of functionalism, consciousness will still supervene on many different implementations, all of which are
assumed to exist within the Plenitude. So it is possible
for an observer to forget enough to become another self
and start life all over again. Perhaps Bhuddists had it
right after all?

8.1.3   Single tracks through Multiverse argument

Some people have suggested that the Multiverse is a bit
like a railway shunting yard. You have a particular worldline which threads its way through the Multiverse. Other
worldlines follow identical histories for a while, but eventually diverge and follow a different history. This is called
differentiation[44]. The fact that other worldlines (or histories) to our own exist is irrelevant to the unfolding of
your own history, which is in effect predetermined. Being
predetermined, the moment of your death is fixed. Any
immortality would be a third person phenomenon, which
is contrary to evidence.

   Such descriptions of reality (David Deutsch is a leading proponent of this idea) are amenable to criticism
by Marchal's movie graph argument, or equivalently
Maudlin's parable of Olympia and Klara (§4.7). All physical processes occupying single predetermined world lines
must be equivalent to a recording of the process. If we
believe conscious processes to supervene on some physical
process, this forces us to conclude that recordings can be
conscious, an absurdity that beggars belief.

   The resolution of the Olympia/Klara parable is that
instead of supervening on a single physical worldline, consciousness must supervene on all identical world lines.
Where the Multiverse differentiates, the first person experience is indeterminate. The whoie quantum immortality

argument is recovered.

8.1.4 Doomsday argument

Jacques Mallah proposed another important counter argument to QTI. It is based on the Doomsday argument introduced in §5.2, but using Bostrom's strong self sampling assumption. The strong self sampling assumption differs from the regular self sampling assumption in stating that one should reason as though one's current *observer moment* (§4.4) were selected randomly. He argues that if QTI were true, then we should expect the combined measure of observer moments with age greater than 200 years old (say) to greatly outweigh those observer moments with ages less than 200 years. This follows as for every observer moment at say age 30, QTI asserts an observer moment exists for age 200, 1000 and so on. Therefore, there are many more observer moments older than 200, than younger, so we should expect to find ourselves older than 200 years of age, conflicting with observational evidence.

Of course this argument simplistically asserts that each observer moment has a measure that is somehow identical, what would be called a uniform measure. John Leslie argued that a uniform measure on observer moments leads to the expectation of us experiencing being moments from death[76]. It would be more reasonable to suppose that any such absolute observer moment measure diminishes with age, roughly proportional to the exponential of the knowledge (complexity) contained within that observer moment. This measure needs then to be multiplied by the number of observer moments having the same age. It is unclear, though, whether this weighting of the measure suffices to rescue QTI from Mallah's critique. Also it is unclear what effect having complex measure would have on the argument, as this is what we'd expect the measure to be (see §4.5).

One possible approach (again assuming positive measure) is to assume that the absolute measure is given by the product of the probabilities (7.2) of all measurements taken by the observer since birth. By virtue of unitarity, the sum of this measure over all observer moments of a given age, must be a declining function of age, with the rate of decline given by the absolute mortality, as a function of age.

The Doomsday argument with selection of observer moments made according to a monotonically declining function of age would predict the youngest of observer moments to be selected. By this argument, it is actually mysterious why we should ever observe ourselves as adults, a reductio ad absurdum for the Mallah argument.

This mystery goes away if we suppose that we have passed through observer moments for all ages less than our current age, as we must do if the TIME postulate were true.

8.2   Absolute vs Relative Self Sampling Assumption

In the course of a lengthy, and at times heated debate between Jacques Mallah and myself, it became clear we were always arguing from disparate positions[86]. At the heart of our difference of opinion was how the strong self sampling assumption should be applied. Jacques Mallah assumed that each observer moment had an absolute positive measure, and that our current observer moment is selected at random from that distribution.

Since I accept the TIME postulate, only the birth moment is selected at random, according to the self sampling assumption. Thereafter, each observer moment's measure can be determined *relative* to its predecessor by means of Born's rule (7.2). Arguing with this notion of observer measure, first person immortality follows provided the no cul-de-sac conjecture is true.

The Everything List adopted the term *Absolute Self Sampling Assumption* to refer to Mallah's use of strong self sampling, and the *Relative Self Sampling Assumption* for the version I use. Since this debate took place, other debates have taken place between members of the "absolute" camp, which includes such names as Jacques Mallah, Saibal Mitra, Hal Finney and the "relative" camp which includes Bruno Marchal, Stathis Papaioannou, and myself.

Both of these "camps" appear to have internally consistent pictures. The fact that I'm not currently experiencing childhood, is for me strong evidence that the ASSA is an incorrect application of the strong self sampling assumption.

8.3 Applications of Quantum Immortality

In the Multiverse, anything possible does happen in some world. Winning the lottery is one future state of purchasing a lottery ticket. Is there a way of ensuring the experience of winning the lottery? What about coupling our survival to the winning ticket?

Think of the following thought experiment. Create a machine coupled to the media channels used to announce the outcome of the lottery. A ticket is purchased, and the ticket number is fed into the machine. The machine is programmed to kill the occupant of the machine when the lottery results are announced unless the purchased ticket

matches the winning ticket. By the logic of the quantum
theory of immortality, anyone using this machine will be
first person guaranteed of winning the lottery. Too bad
for their families and friends left behind! This idea is
called *quantum suicide*.

Could such a machine actually work? There are very
significant practical difficulties in getting it to work. Most
lotteries have a winning chance of several tens of millions to one. Most methods of death have a substantially
higher failure rate than this. The chance of surviving being shot with a gun at point blank range is most likely
greater than one in a hundred, which is *five orders of
magnitude* more likely than winning the lottery. If a gun
aimed at your head was your chosen method of disposal,
then waking up in hospital the day after with a hole in
your head is much more likely than winning the lottery.
Of course, with engineering, it is possible to reduce failure rates. One considers likely modes of failure, builds
redundant systems to remove those modes of failure, and
repeat. However, reducing the failure rate by the ten orders of magnitude or so needed to win the lottery is an
engineering feat without precedent. Such an engineering
project would probably vastly exceed the expected win-
nings in terms of cost! So please don't try this at home.

Has anyone actually tried quantum suicide? The
thought experiment is so appealing, that someone might
be tempted to try it without thinking through the practi-
calities. In fact one contributer to the Everything List ad-
mitted to trying quantum suicide[4]. He built a machine in
much the manner described above, with several guns for
added redundancy. What happened? As it turned out, he
fell in love! As a consequence he couldn't go through with
the act. From this experience he drew a rather interest-

---

[4]I will discreetly not mention his name

ing conclusion that something less improbable would happen to interfere with quantum roulette situations. Such an effect would require a modification of the RSSA to something that includes a "reverse causality"[87] component.[5] Such an effect would also presumably prevent cul-de-sac states from being entered, thus rescuing QTI even if such states existed. I'm somewhat sceptical of this reverse causality idea however — it does seem contrary to standard quantum mechanics.

Active quantum suicide as above is a selfish act, if not morally repugnant. Performing the act would probably turn friends and family against you, if they were aware of you doing it. The most likely outcome is consigning yourself to an eternal lifetime of solitude and loneliness. You could call this the "curse of King Midas".

However, we are engaged in a sort of quantum suicide anyway, just by living our everyday life. This is particularly true as we age. We can exploit the structure of superannuation to our advantage. A lifetime pension plan offers an almost infinite return[6] to a consumer experiencing immortality. For the insurance company, the *expected* payout can be computed by *actuarial data*, and premiums adjusted so that the company can make a profit. It is a win-win situation for consumers and insurance companies alike.

This is a passive approach to using quantum immortality, and is a strategy that most people would be happy

---

[5]Similar sorts of effects are often proposed to counteract the grandfather paradox of time travel — something will always happen to prevent you going back in time and killing your grandfather before he had a chance to father your mother (or father as the case may be). Of course in the Multiverse, the grandfather paradox disappears — see [43] for an explanation.

[6]Limited only by the lifetime of the insurance company, which will be finite, of course.

to accept. A more active approach to pensions was suggested by James Higgo[63], whereby Governments could educate pensioners in the quantum theory of immortality, and offer all pensioners an increase in their pension provided that they commit quantum suicide. I doubt whether James was being entirely serious though, as he does quote from Jonathon Swift's "A modest proposal", one of Swift's most famous satires.

8.4   Decision Theory

It has been asked numerous times on the Everything list whether knowledge of the quantum theory of immortality might affect behaviour. There have been surprisingly few examples offered by people, perhaps because in many ways there is little to distinguish the Multiverse from simply having multiple possible futures. Here are a few areas I feel it makes a difference.

The first is the issue of taking out lifetime pension, which I mentioned in the previous section. With an expectation of first person immortality, lifetime pension seems like a very good deal, if not essential to avoid poverty during a vast era of decrepitude. Unfortunately, insurance companies have only a finite expected lifetime, no firm will avoid bankruptcy forever. You will eventually be forced to rely on the good will of others to support you.

The second issue is that of euthanasia. At first blush, the appeal of euthanasia is to end suffering. But how could it do that if the suffering person has first person immortality? The euthanased person may no longer be in your world, in your life, but would nevertheless be experiencing continued suffering in another universe, if not greater suffering because of your actions. This for me, is a powerful argument against euthanasia.

The third issue I can think of relates to personal conduct, whether you decide to be a kind, altruistic kind of person, or a mean, selfish one. Many religions offer the prospect of an eternal afterlife, with a rewarding afterlife if you are good, and a punishing one if you are bad. Quantum immortality, I believe, generates the same sort of incentives. Belief in a real death, one that terminates your existence, offers you an escape route, and might encourage one to be selfish if one's gains outweighed the short term unpopularity. Even the offer of salvation would serve as an escape route here. St. Augustine famously deferred baptism until he was 33 so he could continue his enjoyment of the pleasures of the flesh. "Give me chastity and contingency, only not yet."[7, Book 8, §7.17]. However, the prospect of personal immortality closes this escape route. You have a choice of an eternal life in "heaven" or in "hell", depending on how you treat your fellow people. We are a strongly social species. Altruism in humans is strictly enforced by a system of reciprocal altruism and punishment. The extent to which humans are prepared to punish others who don't toe the line has been recently discovered by Ernst Fehr and Dominique de Quervain[38]. If you are kind to others, that kindness will be repaid, not necessarily by the person you help, but by another person who was helped by another, etc. in a kind of loop to the person you originally helped. Such loops are likely to be small, due to the *small world* structure of human relationships[144], i.e. the "six degrees of separation". Conversely, of course, being mean encourages others to do the same, and you end up creating a kind of hell for yourself.

A critic of this view would object that in the Multiverse, there would be a version of you that is evil anyway, a mass murderer perhaps, and that the proportion of your copies that are good and evil is simply a characteristic of your personality. Nothing you can do changes the deterministic nature of the Multiverse. I will argue in the next chapter that free will really does exist, and is not an "illusion" as commonly asserted — in the deterministic Multiverse. Consequently, you can choose whether to live in a "heaven" or "hell", we are not just passive passengers on the train of life.

Quantum immortality is thus a very good incentive to behave altruistically, a grounding for the *golden rule* of Christianity: "Do unto others that which you would have done to you". Of course Christians do not have a monopoly on altruism — altruism is a basic feature of the human species, and it tends to be reinforced by most of humanity's belief systems. Human societies are limited by the amount of *cheating* (which is evolutionarily inevitable), so systems like *punishment, religion* and *justice* evolve to suppress the level of cheating, and enable larger societies to exist.

8.5   More Possible Immortality Scenarios

Probably the most likely scenario for the experience of immortality in our lifetimes is through advances in medicine keeping us alive longer and healthier. This leads to scenarios of increasing use of prosthetics, the "cyborgisation" of the human species.

A somewhat more extreme futurist's prediction relates to the increasing capability of computing technology. For the last 40 years, computers have been doubling in performance every 18 months, an observation dubbed *Moore's law*. Over 40 years, this amounts to a hundred million fold improvement in computing performance. Whilst much has been written about possible limits to Moore's law, there is no actual "show stopper" preventing this technological improvement to continue indefinitely. Once computers become powerful enough to design themselves without the need of human creativity, technological improvement will accelerate, leaving Moore's law far behind, so much so that an infinite amount of computational power is reached in a finite amount of time. Of course, an infinite amount of computation is impossible, what it does tell us is that our current conceptions will break down — a technological *singularity*.[73] Vernor Vinge develops the argument that this could happen *within 30 years*.[143, 154] Once singularity is reached, it is possible that our minds will be uploaded, that we will become part of an immortal superintelligence.

If we accept the premise of *computationalism*, it is possible that we are living in a simulation, in the style of the move *Matrix*. Just as we wake up from a nightmare before being killed, we might suddenly wake up from what we know as life just prior to experiencing death. What world we wake into, we can only speculate — but it could as easily be a traditional religious notion of afterlife, Heaven or Hell perhaps, as anything else.

Chapter 9

Consciousness and Free Will

> Time is an illusion. Lunch time doubly so.
> *Douglas Adams*

9.1 Illusions

Illusion is a pretty strong word. Stage magicians use illusion to convince an audience they are seeing a physical impossibility unfolding before their eyes — *illusion* connotes *deception* of the senses. Of course the individuals themselves may not be deceived. Most rational people do not actually think that the stage magician has really performed a physically impossible act, however their senses are deceived in the the sense of not seeing how the conjuror did the trick.

Philosophers use the word illusion a lot. Time is an illusion[99], Free will is an illusion[145], or in a recent New Scientist article discussing Bell's theorem "Free Will or Reality, one of these is an illusion... but which?"[23]. It is used so often, and as oxymorons like "Reality is an illusion", that I wonder if *illusion* means something different in the field of philosophy to everyday usage. If so, then what does illusion mean in a philosophical context?

Imagine tying a weight (eg a stone) to a string, and then twirl around, like a hammer thrower at the Olympic Games. You probably conducted this experiment for real during your childhood — if not, you are welcome to try it, so long as you leave plenty of space around you in case the weight comes off. The string will stretch taut, as though there is something invisible pulling on the weight at the end of the string. This phenomenon goes by the name *centrifugal force*, which literally means "centre fleeing". In high school physics, I was taught that centrifugal force is an illusion, no such force actually exists. Taking a bird's eye view on the twirling weight, we can see that the weight is constantly accelerating towards the centre by a force due to the tension in the string — without this force the weight would travel in a straight line, as predicted by Newton's first law of motion. Such a force is called a *centripetal force* ("centre seeking"). There is no centrifugal force acting in the opposite direction.

Later in my physics career, I learnt of the concept of *inertial reference frame*. In Newtonian dynamics, an inertial reference frame is the point of view of an observer travelling at a constant velocity with respect to any other inertial reference frame. Newton's first law applies in any inertial reference frame, and there will be a unique reference frame for which the object is at rest. In the case of the spinning weight, however, the weight is only at rest in a rotating reference frame, which is noninertial, ie a reference frame that is accelerating with respect to an inertial reference frame. To keep something like Newton's first law applicable in this frame, our brains posit an extra force, called a *pseudo force* to counter the obvious tension force of the string, and keep the weight immobile.

This notion of reference frame is extended to General Relativity, in which spacetime is curved near massive bodies. Newton's first law is modified to bodies travelling along *geodesics* if not acted upon by any force. A geodesic is a minimal length path between any two points, which in general is not a straight line (it is only straight in flat spacetime). Our brain posits a pseudo force to explain the departure of the geodesic trajectory from the straight line that is expected from our naive understanding of Newton's first law. This pseudo force is called *gravity*. In fact, in a falling lift, or in orbit, we are in general relativity's version of an inertial reference frame, and in these situations we experience weightlessness, or an absence of gravity. It would be absurd to call gravity an illusion (in my opinion at least), equally it is just as absurd to call centrifugal force an illusion. However, it is important to recognise them as properties of a point of view, not of some objective reality that is "out there" somewhere.

In §2.3, we discussed the second law of thermodynamics, and how its appearance depends on the observer. From the point of view of us mortal humans, a thermodynamic system is well modelled by just a few macroscopic quantities, such as temperature and pressure. The thermodynamic model has a quantity called entropy that never decreases in time, but can increase. This model is *irreversible*. However, from the point of view of Laplace's daemon, who knows the precise positions and momenta of all particles making up the system, the system is reversible, as all the equations describing the motions of the particles are all reversible. Should we therefore say that the second law of thermodynamics is an illusion, caused by our limited perceptual capabilities? Again, I believe this is absurd, an abuse of terminology.

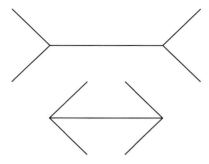

Figure 9.1: Müller-Lyer illusion. The center lines in each figure are of identical length

What about the term *emergence* that is generally accepted as a label for how irreversible dynamics arises out of reversible dynamics? I gave a detailed description in §2.1 of what I mean by emergence, a concept often called weak emergence. Recapping a little, where one has two descriptions of a phenomenon, and one description uses concepts not reducible to the other, these concepts are *emergent*. This seems like a perfect fit for pseudo forces, where the two levels of description are the "at-rest" reference frame, which has pseudo forces, and any inertial reference frame which doesn't have any such pseudo forces.

Perhaps whenever a philosopher uses the term "illusion", and is not talking about real illusions such as the classic Müller-Lyer illusion shown in figure 9.1, this philosopher really means emergence.

To apply the notion of emergence to discussions of consciousness, we need to fix the two levels of description that we called syntactic and semantic in §2.1. We can distinguish between the internal, or subjective point of view of something, or how it appears to the observer, and the external, or objective point of view of that something. Kant talks about *phenomenon*, or the appearance of something, and *noumenon* or the thing in itself[1]. Max Tegmark uses animal imagery, in the form of the *frog perspective*, to refer to the perspective of an observer embedded in a parallel universe ensemble, and the *bird perspective* to refer to a hypothetical view across all universes in the ensemble[134].

Another way of talking about these perspectives is as the "external" and "internal" perspectives, where the internal/external relationship is relative to the conscious observer. We can also distinguish between the internal view of external phenomena (ie the world, or universe in a Multiverse), and the internal view of internal phenomena (consciousness and the like).

In keeping with Bruno Marchal's usage, however, I will use the terms *first person* and *third person* perspectives to refer to these points of view. A phenomenon in the first person perspective, that doesn't have a direct correlate with something in the third person perspective is clearly emergent. A *materialist*,[2] someone who states that a concrete reality exists, might be inclined dismiss anything that wasn't directly represented in the third person perspective as a mere "illusion", something not worthy of objective science. By contrast an *idealist* would be more inclined to attribute primacy to 1st person experiences. Starting with René Descartes' famous dictum *Cogito ergo sum*, they would argue that we can only trust direct experiences, inferring the third person world from consistencies amongst observations, and amongst reports from other observers.

---

[1]The German phrase used by Kant "*Ding an sich*", meaning *thing in itself* is often used in this context

[2]I'll have more to say about various 'isms pervading this field later

As may be appreciated, this book has an idealist flavour. In chapter 7, I've argued that the basic equations of physics can be deduced from the process of observation. There is perhaps no evidence of a concrete external reality at all, or putting it another way that the concrete reality is Nothing, the Plenitude of all descriptions described in §3.2. So how do we define what is meant by third person perspective? In the absence of a concrete reality, we can define the first person plural perspective as that part of the first person perspective shared by multiple observers. For instance, you and I might agree we are looking at a brown dog (first person plural), but neither of us know whether we share the same perception of brown (pure first person phenomenon known as *qualia*). In the limit, we can consider the third person perspective as that shared by all possible observers. We know from §7.1 that this must be a subset of the Everett Multiverse, so for the rest of this chapter, we will use the Multiverse to stand in for the third person perspective. However, as observers embedded within the Multiverse, we do not see the whole Multiverse, but rather one of the "worlds", or "branches" within the Multiverse. Phenomena directly accessible to all observers within a particular branch corresponds to what most people might call objective physics, or reality.

Bruno Marchal also introduces the concept of the communicable and incommunicable parts of a Löbian machine's knowledge. By communicable, Bruno means that not only does a machine know something to be true, but can also prove it (to another person). As an example of incommunicable knowledge, he invokes his parable of someone undergoing a brain transplant with an appropriately programmed computer. An external observer can verify that the transplantee behaves identically after the operation as before, yet can never know whether it is still the *same* person on the inside.

9.2 Time

Let's think about the sentence "Time is an illusion". This
doesn't mean that there isn't a direction in spacetime that
can't be labelled "time"[3]. What it is referring to is the
impression that time "flows" from future, to present to
past.

In §4.3, I propose that this *psychological time*, a sense
of "now", which turns into the past, and of future events
turning into the "now", is an essential ingredient both
in the explanation of why the universe remains orderly,
and also in the derivation of quantum mechanics. This
assumption I label TIME.

The concept of *observer moment* was introduced in
§4.4. Intuitively it corresponds the smallest possible conscious experience, a moment in time. Between any two
observer moments, there is possibly an accessibility relation. If that is the case we say that one observer moment
is a successor of the other. If we select a chain of such
observer moments (each observer moment connected to a
single sucessor moment), we have an ordered set that is
our psychological time. TIME states that we consciously
experience such a chain of observer moments, one after
the other.

Clearly this psychological time is not part of the third
person perspective. The third person perspective is a network of observer moments, with no ordering and no flow

---

[3]In fact any direction will do, so long as the displacement in
that direction according the the Minkowski formula (7.3) is a real
number. Such displacements are termed *timelike*, and if the displacement is an imaginary number, (proportional to $\sqrt{-1}$), the displacement is called *spacelike*.

of time. It is, as David Deutsch calls, a *block Multiverse*, a fixed arrangement of experiences. Psychological time, as we assumed with TIME, is a necessary part of the 1st person perspective in order for the Multiverse to emerge in the third person.

Consciousness is also an emergent phenomenon. It exists entirely in the first person perspective, yet by the Anthropic Principle, it supervenes on (or emerges out of) first person plural phenomena. So psychological time, being a property of consciousness is, also emergent. This is actually quite a conventional view of consciousness in the field of complex systems theory[52], but it kind of sweeps the mind-body problem under the rug. Consciousness would appear to be relegated to a mere epiphenomenon, with no causal influence over reality, at least if strong emergence were denied.

However, we also have the third person world emerging out of consciousness, just as explained in §7.1. The Anthropic Principle cuts both ways — reality must be compatible with the conscious observer, and the conscious observer must supervene on reality. This leads to an emergence "loop", of the type predicted by Ian Stewart and Jack Cohen[132].[4] These loops are called *strange loops* — an idea expounded in Hofstadter's *Gödel, Escher, Bach*[65].

For some people, a causal loop is a sign of a fatal flaw in a theory. Dictionaries for example will give definitions that depend on other definitions that depend in turn on the original definition, what are called *circular definitions*. This sort of thing is frowned upon in a mathematical or logical theory — theorems should be derivable from a limited set of propositions, the axioms, that are assumed true a priori. Nevertheless, circular defini-

---

[4]and is an example of downward causation

tions do not make dictionaries useless for determining the meanings of words. There will probably be sufficient information in an English dictionary for someone to learn the English language (given enough effort on their part) without knowing the meanings of a single English word beforehand. That babies can bootstrap their knowledge of language from a position of knowing no words at all indicates this possibility at least.

To put the boot on the other foot, let us examine alternatives to circularly causal systems: Either we have a chain of causality termintaing in some *first cause* (often identified as God), or the chain continues as an *infinite regression* — "turtles all the way down".[5] None of these options, which exhaust the set of possibilities, has a clear advantage over the others.

9.3 Self Awareness

In §5.1, we concluded that self-awareness is another necessary feature of consciousness, if for no other reason than to prevent the collapse under Occam's razor to a trivial environment. Self awareness also has another desirable property. Since our observed reality must contain our "body"[6] in order for us to be self-aware, and since this reality must be otherwise as simple as possible by Occam's razor, we can deduce by the arguments in chapter

---

[5]It is somewhat of an urban legend that a famous scientist (eg Bertrand Russell or Thomas Huxley) was once challenged by a little old lady who claimed the world was flat and supported on the back of a tortoise. The scientist, wishing to discredit this thesis, asked her on what the tortoise stood. "It's turtles all the way down" was the response.

[6]In philosophical discussions of the mind-body problem, the body includes the brain and anything else that is physically part of us. The mind may or may not be part of the body — that's the problem!

6 that our body must arise by means of an evolutionary process. This latter observation has some interesting
consequences. Evolution requires variation upon which
to act. Variation amongst individuals implies we're not
alone, so implies at very least the appearance of other
conscious observers.

I have argued in this book that our observed reality
is constructed by means of observing a randomly selected
bitstring from the ensemble of all such bitstrings. The
Anthropic Principle implies that part of this bitstring describes our body, as well as other people's bodies. There
are two ways of interpreting this finding:

1. That the descriptions are just descriptions of an unknowable reality located somewhere else. Our real
   bodies are located in this unknowable reality, and
   what we observe are mere "tokens" of this unknowable reality. Why our observations should have any
   bearing on this reality is a fundamental mystery.
   This way leads to *solipsism*, or the belief that there
   is no external reality, and only one observer exists.
   This way suffers from the Occam catastrophe (§5.1).
   Alternatively, we can take Bishop Berkley's rescue
   package, which sees God as taking infinite care to
   align experience with the unknowable reality. This
   latter option, an appeal to a mysterious and all powerful being, is worse in my opinion, than simply
   assuming there is an ultimately unexplainable concrete reality within which we exist.

2. That a description logically capable of observing
   itself is enough to bootstrap itself into existence.
   Let me speak to this by means of an example: The
   C programming language is a popular language for
   computer applications. To convert a program writ-

ten in C into machine instructions that can execute on the computer, one uses another program called a compiler. Many C compilers are available, but a popular compiler is the GNU C compiler, or gcc. Gcc is itself a C language program, you can download the program source code from http://www.gnu.org, and compile it yourself, if you already have a working C compiler. Once you have compiled gcc, you can then use gcc to compile itself. Thus gcc has bootstrapped itself onto your computer, and all references to any preexisting compiler forgotten.

What I'm tryng to say here is that the description is a complete specification of a conscious being, when interpreted (observed) by the conscious being. There may have been an initial interpreter (conscious or not) to bootstrap the original conscious being. It matters not which interpreter it is — any suitable one will do. If *computationalism* §4.7 is correct, any universal Turing machine will suffice. In fact since the third person world has to be a timeless *ideal* structure, it is not necessary to actually run the initial interpreter. The logical possibility of a conscious observer being able to instantiate itself is sufficient in a timeless Plenitude of all possibilities. Thus we close the ontology of the bitstring Plenitude, and find an answer to Stephen Hawking's question "What breathes fire into the equations"[59, p. 174]. Paraphrasing the words of Pierre-Simon Laplace to Napoleon Bonaparte, we have no need of a hypothesis of a concrete reality[94].

Bruno Marchal devotes a whole chapter to demolishing the requirement of a concrete reality in his thesis within the assumption of *computationalism*[94]. The argument I give above is non-formal, "hand-waving" version of this argument, which appears to work with a more general set of assumptions than *computationalism*. I have not at this point in time worked exactly what is needed to make it work, however I do expect that conscious observers will be found to be capable of universal computation (and perhaps more).

Now if we accept that a description capable of observing and instantiating itself is conscious, then we must also conclude that other descriptions of things capable of observing and instantiating themselves must also be conscious. Thus no zombies[7].

Furthermore, since the Anthropic Principle applies equally to the other observers in our reality, as it does to us, the first person plural physics observed by them will also be identical to ours. This explains the consistency of the first person plural perspective.

9.4 Free Will

Free will is one of those topics, like the nature of consciousness, that generates a lot of traffic on email discussion lists like the Everything list, and the Fabric of Reality list, without much of substance being discussed. So what I want to do here is present my own very partisan view of free will. I will trot out the usual counter arguments raised against my position, to which I will take the author's privelege of having last right of reply. I won't

---

[7]A zombie in philosophical discussions does not refer to half dead slave of some voodoo priest, but to an entity that is to all respects indistinguishable from a fully conscious person, but is in fact unconscious. This is another example of a word that has a different meaning in philosophical discussion than everyday life.

spend much time discussing competing views of the nature of free will. What I hope to demonstrate is that consideration of the Multiverse adds something new and substantial to the ongoing debate on free will.

Let me first go on the record and say what I think I mean by free will: *It is the ability for a conscious entity to do something irrational.* Computers are the archetypal rational beings — assuming a well-posed and above all solvable problem, a computer applies an algorithm and determines the unique best solution. The trouble is that there are many more intractable, if not ill-posed problems in the day-to-day business of just surviving, than there are tractable ones. Such a rational entity as our computer example would not solve these problems, but instead get caught in an endless loop, and would not pass the survival test that most animals pass with flying colours each day of their lives. It is interesting to note that in the last thirty years, biologically inspired computing has lead to algorithms that use a controlled amount of irrationality (in the form of randomness or pseudorandomness), and these have been used with significant success at solving previously intractable computational problems in a diverse range of applications. So instead of being stupid, being irrational is sometimes very smart.

Perhaps the biggest impact the Multiverse has on the free will debate comes from Maudlin's construction of Olympia (§4.7). Recall that Olympia was little more than a recording of how a hypothetical conscious computer Klara behaved during a particular epoch of a deterministic universe. In a single deterministic universe, we can replay Olympia with all the original inputs from the deterministic universe, and Olympia is physically indistinguishable from Klara. However, in a Multiverse, not only is our original universe present, but also all the counterfactual universes as well. Clearly from the third person perspective, Klara and Olympia as as different as chalk and cheese. In a Multiverse, a mere recording cannot be conscious.

Now consider another construction, called the *Huge Look Up Table* (HLUT). This consists presenting all possible inputs to Klara (assumed finite), and recording Klara's response. The HLUT will be indistinguishable from Klara across the Multiverse, but is it conscious? Various people respond differently to this question. Computationalists would have to answer yes, as they assert Klara is conscious. People who are persuaded by John Searle's *Chinese Room argument* would be inclined to say no — a lookup table can never be conscious. I will remain seated on the fence here. Such a lookup table would be astronomically huge, rather beyond mortal comprehension — things with large numbers have the habit of behaving qualitatively different to smaller versions of the same thing.

However, I would argue that neither the HLUT, nor Klara has free will (as I have defined it above), nor, I suspect, might it even have the "illusion" of free will. For every possible input, these machines produce a unique output. By contrast, the human brain seems designed from the outset to exploit sources of randomness (§6.2) at the synaptic level, i.e. to behave a little irrationally from time to time.

It is clear that this occasional irrationality is the basis of human creativity[8]. It is also has other uses in an

---

[8]This is not a substantive reason — most of the animal kingdom gets by with little or no creativity. The exceptions are all the more remarkable, eg the New Caledonian crow called Betty that fashioned a hook from a length of wire, even though her species has no experience with materials resembling wires in the natural environment[147].

evolutionary setting. In the phenomenon of *predator con-fusion*, a group of prey animals (eg herd of antelope, or a school of fish) will often outwit the predator by darting about at random. Even in a one-on-one contest, a prey animal attempting to evade a predator can exploit randomness, making it difficult for the predator to predict the movement of prey.

So yes it is free, but is it will? The usual counterargument given is why should mere randomness in behaviour have anything to do with having causal influence on the world, in other words, with having a will. One is just prisoner of a different prison, a prisoner of chance, rather than rigid certainty. A second flavour of this type of argument hinges on the concept of responsibility: perhaps "My synapses made me do it, your honour" will be submitted as a defense in a criminal court. I shall leave the notion of responsibility to its own section, and for now just focus on how free will is compatible with chance behaviour.

The first point is that I'm not claiming free will to be a phenomenon in the third person world, or even of the first person plural world (although indeterminancy is). It is an emergent concept whose utility is in understanding and predicting the actions of other people. Therefore the traditional move arguing that free will (or consciousness for that matter) is not needed to explain the objective world, and is hence is an "illusion" is invalid. As stated previously, one could equally argue that the second law of thermodynamics is an illusion.

9.5 Why self-awareness and free will?

We have argued for the emergence of self-awareness and free will. This solves the problem of how these concepts can be compatible with worlds completely specified by entities that have neither property without invoking a separate spiritual world in the style of Descartes. The emergence of life from appropriate configurations of nonliving matter similarly eliminates *vitalism*. However, there remains the question of just what these things are for. Life exists because it can — it exists as patterns able to reproduce themselves, and to evolve. Consciousness also exists because it can. However what *evolutionary* reasons exist for consciousness to evolve? Why should creatures evolve that are aware of themselves in the environment, and why should they feel *in charge*?

Dennett gives a very interesting reason in *Consciousness Explained*[41]. Human brains evolved by a multiplication of specialist brain circuits solving specific problems of survival in the animal world. Humans are generalists, and are often faced with problems that are unlike any previously solved. The solution will most likely involve novel combinations of existing solutions, but how to solve the problem of connecting the existing solution scattered throughout the brain. He uses the metaphor of Plato's aviary, with the problem of how to call the right bird into one's hand. And the answer, according to Dennett, is a "clever trick", called *autostimulation*. Once humans obtained the use of language, every time they uttered a word, all sorts of related, ancilliary concepts are retrieved. A popular game (and sometimes serious psychological research tool) is *word association*. In this game, a questioner says a sequence of words, with the responder responding with whatever first came into er mind. The object is to deduce something about the responder's psychological structure from the associations. Anyway, the point Dennett makes is that this trick allows ideas to be connected via this word association, that would otherwise be segregated within the "chapels of the mind" (to use Steven Mithen's term[100]). Once this trick was learnt, it is clear that the physical speech would be optimised away, leading to an internal narrative, or Joycean *stream of consciousness*. "Speaking" to oneself implies awareness of oneself.

An alternative explanation for self-awareness comes from a theory called *Machiavellian Intelligence*[151, 24]. Named after Niccolò Machiavelli, who wrote a famous political treatise called *The Prince*, the theory describes the evolutionary advantage for group living individuals to deceive their colleagues in order to obtain power and privelege. Ethologists Peter Driver and David Humphries noticed that many animals develop cognitive capacities so that they can predict the actions of their competitors or prey. Natural selection then favours mechanisms that make these actions harder to predict, so their enemies evolve better predictive powers, and an evolutionary arms race develops.

Geoffrey Miller argued that in social species such as human beings, outwitting fellow humans is more important than other animals[47]. There are two aspects to this: the first is a selection pressure to attempt to predict other members of our species, and the second a competing pressure to avoid being predictable by other members of our species. To predict what other people do, we need a *theory of the mind*, a model of human minds that predicts other people's actions. And what more economical way of obtaining a model of the mind, but to observe our own mind at work. The immediate consequence of this is self-awareness. And what better way to avoid being too predictable than to exploit the chaotic dynamics in the brain (see §6.2). It pays to do the irrational thing sometimes. With self-awareness, any actual departure from one's own model of behaviour will appear as a freedom of will. Even when you act rationally, the knowledge that you could have acted otherwise generates the feeling of free will.

Self-awareness and free will are two sides of the same coin, a consequence of an evolutionary arms race between intelligent animals living in a social group.

These two arguments provide rather different conclusions when faced with the question of non-human consciousness. Dennett's autostimulation theory, with its emphasis on language, pretty much rules out consciousness in any other animal other than ourselves. Coupling this with Steven Mithen's theories on the evolution of the human mind[100], we can only conclude that consciousness appeared with a burst in our species around 40,000 years ago, well after our species had spread to every corner of the globe.

The Machiavellian Intelligence idea would point to a more generous inclusion of non-human consciousness. We should expect that consciousness will only arise in highly social species, where competition between individuals is an important force of selection (ruling out the eusocial insects for instance). With this idea, most of the great apes are probably conscious, as are bottlenose dolphins. Doubtless a few other species will be found to exhibit complex social interactions, as well as demonstrate self awarenss. Dogs, for example, constitute a borderline case. A social species in the wild, with "pack politics", dogs do not pass the mirror test. This may be because the olfactory world is more important to a dog than the visual, or it may be that dogs have not learnt the "trick" of consciousness. Regardless of which evolutionary explanation is found to be valid, I can conclude in agreement with Dennett that consciousness is an extremely rare property in the animal kingdom.

9.6 Responsibility

The other argument usually advanced against the stochastic interpretation of free will is that you could plead lack of responsibility in a court of law, as your actions are simply due to chance events. This is usually presented as saying indeterminate behaviour is no more free will than completely determined behaviour. It's a 'my synapses made me do it" versus "my genes made me do it" argument.

Let me state this quite boldly: the notion of legal responsibility has nothing whatsoever to do with free will.

Legal responsibility is used for different purposes, depending on whether the case is civil or criminal. In civil cases, legal responsibility decides who pays cost and damages. In criminal cases, it used to decide whether an agent should be punished. An agent here may be a person, or a company, or any other thing that legal tradition recognises as a *legal entitity*. It is particularly poignant that the responsible entity need not be a person, and can be something we don't normally associate with free will.

In criminal cases, the purpose of punishment is to prevent that occurrence from happening again. Human society depends on punishment to ensure altruism[38]. If the agent is a learning system, then applying punishment to the agent can cause the agent to learn — the stick of "carrot and stick". Alternatively, the punishment could be used to deter others from committing the same crime. In the worst case scenario, an incorrigible person might be imprisoned for life, or even executed, if they were a danger to society.

The notion of diminished responsibility is an inter-

esting case. Here, an agent may be found to be under
the influence of another agent, so one can attribute some
of the responsibility to another agent. However, as the
Nürnberg trials showed, this is a very shaky defence. It
cannot be applied to the sources of randomness within
your brain — those sources of randomness are still part
of the legal entity that is you. Nor could it be applied
to your genes. It only works where you were forced to
perform an act against your will.

If a tumour of the brain caused someone to behave
antisocially, and surgical intervention can cure the so-
ciopathy, it would be quite right for a judge to insist on
the "punishment" of the tumour being removed. It does
not remove legal responsibility from the defendent.

Pleading the defence of insanity can really only alter
the punishment. Punishing an insane person to make
them learn will probably not work — different sort of
treatment, such as psychotherapy might be appropriate.

Having dispatched the legal responsibility argument,
what about moral responsibility? Many religions have
a notion that we are responsible to God, and that free
will is an essential requirement to be held accountable
for our sins. Since I am not a religious person, I have a
hard time being convinced by this line of argument. At
best, I consider morality is a kind of pre-legal notion that
humans evolved to enable social living. For an agent to
function within a society, it must act in certain ways, and
be responsible for its actions if it deviates. This is true,
even if the agents concerned are completely deterministic.

9.7 Interpretations of Quantum Mechanics

A number of interpretations have been developed of quantum mechanics over the years. The *Copenhagen Interpretation* is a blend of Bohr's, Heisenberg's and von Neumann's interpretation, and in fact two different versions of the Copenhagen Interpretation follow depending on whether you follow Bohr (the state vectors, ψ also called wavefunctions, are not real) or Heisenberg (the state vectors are real). If ψ is real, then we have the issue of *wavefunction collapse*, the instantaneous collapse of a universe sized object to a single point, when measuring positions of particles. In the Copenhagen Interpretation, reality is not deterministic.

The *Many Worlds Interpretation* on the other hand also considers ψ to be real, but spread out over multiple worlds in parallel. Reality is deterministic, and wavefunctions do not collapse. However, consider the first person perspective of the Multiverse. We can identify ψ with an observer moment. On performing a measurement, the observer splits into multiple observers, each with a different resulting ψ. This "splitting" happens effectively instantaneously, from the observers point of view, the wavefunction has collapsed. There is no contradiction with relativity though, as it simply involves information changes within the observer, not influences propagating across the universe at the speed of light. Each observer will see a different splitting. By considering the first person point of view as distinct from the third person, the Copenhagen Interpretation is resurrected as the view of the Multiverse *from the inside*.

I should note that other interpretations of quantum mechanics, such as Bohm's pilot wave theory, or the consistent histories interpretation are not so obviously reconcilable.

9.8 Realism

The term *realism*, and associated terms *real* and *reality* crop up a lot in philosophical discussion. Indeed in the everything list, a rather long running thread discussed this issue recently[33]. I think part of the problem with these terms is the tautologous statement: realism is the statement that reality is real. This obviously begs the question of what we mean by "reality". For everyday use, reality refers to the "world beyond our skin", what I have called here the first person plural world. Yet reality may also refer to an ensemble, eg the Multiverse or one of the Plenitude's discussed in chapter 3. *Platonic realism* is the name given to Plato's idea that *ideals* really exist, and what we see are but shadows, or approximations to these ideals. The word *real* is often simply used to add some authority to an argument — for instance the Many Worlds Interpretation can be summed as saying that the other possible worlds are equally as real as our own.

It is clear that the term realism then has little currency. As a consequence, I have deliberately avoided using it, and when using the term reality I will state which reality I am talking about, as several incommensurable realities are operational.

9.9 Other 'isms in Philosophy of the Mind

Australian philosopher David Chalmers is a leading light in the school of thought that consciousness is a "hard problem", completely irreducible, even in principle, to laws of physics. This school of thought has a long history associated with it, going back to Descartes who argued that the unified nature of consciousness is in contradiction with the impossibity of total unity within the world of physics (all things are interconnected to some degree, and boundaries between objects are somewhat a matter of convention). Descartes' solution was *substance dualism*, that conscious minds existed seperately from the physical world, and interacted with the physical world though a point (identified by Descartes as the pineal gland).

Whilst the specific theory proposed by Descartes has long since been abandoned, the ghost of his idea still survives under the notion of dualism, that consciousness cannot be reduced, even in principle, to the laws of physics, and must therefore have a seperate existence.

The notion that physics (including the possibility of physical theories and effects yet to be discovered) is sufficient to explain the phenomenology of consciousness goes by the name of *physicalism*. David Chalmers conflates the terms physicalism and *materialism*[26], whereas Michael Lockwood distinguishes between the two[83]. According to Lockwood, a materialist asserts that consciousness supervenes on the physical world — for every distinct mental state, a distinct physical state must hold. A materialist could accept the possibility of *downward causation*, whereas a physicalist would deny it. The most extreme form of physicalism, the so called *eliminative materialism* denies phenomenal consciousness altogether.

Chalmers's classification scheme includes 3 distinct antimaterialist[9] positions, broadly *interactionism* (type

---

[9]Chalmers's term, although I would argue that these positions only deny the validity of eliminative materialism. Connecting these positions is an acceptance of phenomenal consciousness as a valid

D dualism), *epiphenomenonalism* (type E dualism) and *monism*. Dualism contains not only the traditional substance dualism view of Descartes, but also *emergent* (or property) dualism of the type discussed in §2.1. The distinction between type D and type E dualism is whether downward causation is accepted or not. Finally monism refers to the view that both phenomenal consciousnessness and physics derive from a deeper reality.

Upon reading Chalmers's essay[26], I attempted to fit the theories developed in this book into one of his categories. To be quite frank, they resisted the classification. The Anthropic Principle §5.1 implies supervenience of consciousness on the observed physical world, so in essence it is materialist. Yet the emergence characterisation in §9.2 implies a form of emergence dualism. The existence of causal loops implies a type D dualism. However, one could also argue that it is a form of monism — physics and consciousness are both related to the process of selecting and interpreting descriptions from the Plenitude.

This leads me to suspect that Chalmers has carved the subject up according to past philosophical battles, and undoubtedly that is a valuable contribution in its own right for understanding the history of the subject. I had the opportunity to meet David for lunch, and put this position to him. He denied carving the subject up according to historical divisions, but did admit that alternative classifications were possible. However, nature probably doesn't respect any of the divisions we supply — I have often found such distinctions to be an artifact of the extreme positions some thinkers take, which may seem poles apart as argued, but are really incommensurable descriptions of the same thing. Which leads to my

---

mode of description.

favourite parable of the six blind men and the elephant:

It was six men of Indostan to learning much inclined,
Who went to see the Elephant (though all of them were blind),
That each by observation might satisfy his mind

The First approached the Elephant, and happening to fall
Against his broad and sturdy side, at once began to bawl:
"God bless me! but the Elephant is very like a wall!"

The Second, feeling of the tusk, cried, "Ho! what have we here
So very round and smooth and sharp? to me 'tis mighty clear
This wonder of an Elephant is very like a spear!"

The Third approached the animal, and happening to take
The squirming trunk within his hands, thus boldly up and
spake:
"I see," quoth he, "the Elephant is very like a snake!"

The Fourth reached out an eager hand, and felt about the knee.
"What most this wondrous beast is like is mighty plain," quoth
he;
" 'Tis clear enough the Elephant is very like a tree!?

The Fifth, who chanced to touch the ear, said: "E'en the blin-
dest man
Can tell what this resembles most; deny the fact who can
This marvel of an Elephant is very like a fan!"

The Sixth no sooner had begun about the beast to grope,
Than, seizing on the swinging tail that fell within his scope,
"I see," quoth he, "the Elephant Is very like a rope!"

And so these men of Indostan disputed loud and long,
Each in his own opinion exceeding stiff and strong,
Though each was partly in the right, and all were in the wrong!

Moral:

So oft in theologic wars, the disputants, I ween,
Rail on in utter ignorance of what each other mean,
And prate about an Elephant not one of them has seen!
                                    John Godfrey Saxe

Chapter 10

Summing up

> It is a good morning exercise for a research
> scientist to discard a pet hypothesis every day
> before breakfast. It keeps him young.
>
> Konrad Lorenz

In this book we have looked at what many people think is an outrageous idea, an idea that the reality we see is but a miniscule fragment of the whole. Some would say the notion is obscenely complex, and should be pared away with Occam's razor. They are wrong, of course, ensemble theories of everything turn out to be simpler than the observed fragments. Other people point to Popper, and ask where are the tests? Without the possibility of falsification, a theory is not scientific. Again there are tests for the theory discussed in this book. The Anthropic Principle, or the principle that observed reality must be consistent with the existence of an observer is elevated to a fundamental principle in this theory. The Anthropic Principle can be tested, of course, although nobody really thinks it will be found false. Already, it has been found that the universe is finely tuned to support carbon-based life, our type of consciousness. This is already somewhat miraculous, with people usually accepting either multiple universes, or God as the explanation[1].

However, in the *theory of nothing* proposed in this book, all necessary aspects of observed reality can be linked via the Anthropic Principle to some necessary property of consciousness. Consequently, the development of a theory of consciousness will point to stricter tests of this theory, which can then be carried out by physicists in conjunction with cognitive scientists. I would maintain that this theory *is* scientific in the strict Popperian sense of the word. Furthermore, by accepting the premises of this theory, we can investigate backwards from accepted physical theory (quantum mechanics and general relativity) to find properties of consciousness that need to be valid, in order for that physical theory to be implied. These arguments can then be used to guide a theory of consciousness. We have seen the beginnings of this process in the discussion of the TIME and PROJECTION postulates, as well as the requirement for self-awareness.

There are still further problems raised against theories of this sort. In an ensemble of all possibilities, why should the observed universe continue to remain lawlike? This is the infamous problem of induction, which in the Everything list goes by the name of the *White Rabbit problem*. From evolutionary considerations, we should expect observers to be rather good at extracting patterns from data, and moreover, to be rather robust against noise. White rabbit universes simply do not appear, as they're far too improbable, but less exotic failings of physical law simply go unnoticed.

Secondly, by doing away with any notion of concrete

---

[1]Some people also hope for an explanation in mathematics, that ours is the *only logically possible* universe, but at present there is little evidence that this might be the case.

reality, what, if anything, drives observed phenomena? Is there any external reality at all, or is it all just a dream of a single dreamer? This notion is called solipsism, and solipsism is prevented by the Anthropic Principle. Just as observed phenomena must contain a complete description of the observer, it also must contain complete descriptions of other observers, and this is sufficient to ensure that other observers do exist, and not just appear to exist.

Thus with the main objections disposed of, what advantages accrue? The ontology of bitstrings, with zero complexity, is about as minimal an ontology as you can get. It solves in a stroke, the issue of why anything bothers to exist at all. Along with a small handful of other principles, it seems capable of explaining everything we might want to explain about our existence as conscious observers. These other principles: TIME, PROJECTION, self-awareness and the Anthropic Principle point to a basis for any respectable theory of consciousness.

Finally, what of God? I am not a particularly religious person, so have little motivation, nor am qualified to pursue what consequences the ideas in this book have for theology. However, I'd like to point out one or two things that would be of interest to theologians:

- The ontology of bitstrings has no possible "God's eye" viewpoint. Since the ensemble of bitstrings have zero information, nothing can be learnt from observing it from the outside. This doesn't rule out the possibility of more complex observers than us, in fact somewhere in the Multiverse there are sure to be observers that appear god-like to us. These are more the types of god of the ancient religions — powerful, but not all powerful, knowledgeable beyond our ken, yet not omniscient. Sometimes I say "Demigods yes, but is there room for God?".

- In Schmidhuber's *Religion of the Great Programmer*, a god (the "Great Programmer") instantiates a dovetailer algorithm on some computer somewhere. This god has very little to do, other than to act as a mystical "prime mover". In Marchal's and my philosophies, logical closure obviates the need for even a prime mover.

- Everything necessary in our universe can be traced back to some aspect of our consciousness. We are the creators of our own universes.

- The contrast between internal and external views of the Multiverse reconciles determinism and free will.

- The implication of an eternal life for all, ie the *quantum theory of immortality*, may well justify some aspects of theological doctrine. At very least, the notion that one cannot escape the consequences of one's actions through death is interesting. The small worlds connectivity of social networks implies that altruistic actions will change the social network within which one lives for the good, and that selfish actions change the social networks into mistrusting, spiteful relationships. The choice is yours to live an eternal life in heaven or hell on Earth.

- The traditional notion of life after death is not incompatible with the quantum theory of immortality. At extreme age, or after an extreme trauma like a beheading, nothing short of a miracle can continue conscious experience. Of course such miracles do exist in the Multiverse, which is the basis of quantum immortality. Such a miracle could appear as resurrection into an afterlife. Bear in mind

that such afterlives are white rabbit universes —
any *particular* specification of heaven or hell is very
unlikely to be experienced, but if these descriptions
of heaven and hell are considered as examples, like
our flying, talking white rabbits, or of fire breathing
dragons, rather than as literal truth, then one can
say an afterlife of some sort is a distinct possibility.

- Dementia is also a very likely outcome as one ages.
Some people have suggested that dementia will pro-
ceed to a point where one's experiences are indistinguishable from that of a newborn baby, in which
case the principle of *functionalism* predicts that you
begin life again as a newborn. Thus the idea of reincarnation receives support.

With that my tale has come to an end. From a fairly
conventional physics view of the world, by considering
the role of the observer I was launched into a fantastic
journey through a wonderland, where I seriously started
wondering what, if anything was real. I have had the
privilege to rub minds with some of the brightest of our
times. I have had cause to reexamine some of my most
deeply held beliefs. The results, however have made the
journey well worth the while.

Many puzzling mysteries have fallen away: why *does*
anything bother to exist at all, why are simple and/or
beautiful physical theories more likely to be right and
what does *quantum mechanics* mean. The journey has
taken me into the heart of what David Chalmers calls the
hard problem of consciousness. Whilst I do not claim a solution at this time, the hard problem has certainly broken
down to number of other notoriously baffling problems:
why do we perceive a "flow" of time; how does consciousness select out a single world from the plethora of worlds

available in the Multiverse and why is *self-awareness* necessary for consciousness?

One can at least hope that this is progress!

Appendix A

Basic mathematical ideas used in this book

In his book "A Brief History of Time", Stephen Hawking relays advice given to him that every equation included in a book halves the number of sales. This is a pity, for it makes his book puzzling indeed unless one was already familiar with the material. His description of imaginary time would make no sense if you didn't understand that imaginary means proportional to $\sqrt{-1}$, but instead thought it had the usual English meaning. I do not want to do the same here. There is a time and place for mathematics, when the building blocks of a theory is mathematical. Yet for this book, simple mathematical concepts often suffice — this is not the time and place for mathematical rigour, or for the proof of theorems.

The mathematical concepts used in this book should be familiar to anyone with a solid grounding of mathematics at high school. Yet some of my readers may have missed some parts of necessary mathematics in school, or school may have been so long ago that they're decidedly rusty. I include in this appendix a potted summary of necessary mathematical concepts needed for understanding this book for you convenience. I can recommend the free online encyclopedia Wikipedia[1] for researching these topics in more detail — in mathematics, at least, as well as science Wikipedia has a good reputation for accuracy[54].

A.1 Exponents, logarithms, and functions

You have probably seen expressions like 3^2 (pronounced "three squared") as a shorthand for $3 \times 3 = 9$, and $3^3 = 3 \times 3 \times 3 = 27$ ("three cubed"). The superscripted number is called an exponent. To extract the exponent of a number, we use a function called a logarithm. So $\log_3 9 = 2$ and $\log_3 27 = 3$. The subscripted number (3 in this example) is known as the *base* of the logarithm. One particular number turns out to be an easier base to work with than any other, a number known as e, whose value is approximately $2.7182818\ldots$. Logarithms to base e are called *natural logarithms*, and commonly denoted $\ln x = \log_e x$.

Logarithms obey some very special properties, for instance for any two numbers x and y, the logarithm of the product is the sum of individual logarithms:

$$\log xy = \log x + \log y.$$

Thus a difficult problem (multiplication) is turned into an easy problem (addition) by logarithmic transformation. Logarithm tables, and devices such as slide rules based

---

[1] http://www.wikipedia.org

on logarithms were extremely popular before the advent of electronic calculators.

Just as multiplication is transformed into addition by logarithms, *exponentiation* (raising a number to a power) is transformed into multiplication:

$$\log x^y = y \log x.$$

Just as logarithms to base e enjoy a special status in mathematics, exponentiation of e is also a particularly useful function. We often write

$$\exp(x) = e^x.$$

$\exp(x)$ is called the *exponential function.*

General functions are written $f(x)$, which expresses an association between two values, the argument x, and its value $f(x)$. $\exp(x)$ is an example of such a function, and $\ln(x)$ is another. For some traditional functions such as logarithms and trigonometric functions, the parentheses are optional. Mathematicians often call functions *maps*, as when you map a territory, you associate every point of the territory with some point of the chart.

A.2 Complex numbers

We all know the whole, or natural numbers: 0, 1, 2, ... Negative numbers are what you get when you subtract a bigger number from a smaller one. Rational numbers (also known as fractions) are what you get when you divide one number into another one. Often the result is not a whole number. For example $\frac{3}{2}$ is a rational number that is not a whole number.

The ancient Greeks discovered that not all lengths were a rational number of units (eg centimetres). For

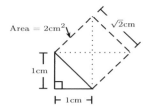

Figure A.1: The hypotenuse of a right angle triangle with unit sides is $\sqrt{2}$, which is an irrational number.

example, a right angle triangle (where one angle is $90°$) with two sides 1cm long has its third side exactly $\sqrt{2}$cm long (see Figure A.1). $\sqrt{2}$ is not a rational number — which can be proven by showing that assuming $\sqrt{2}$ is a rational number leads to a contradiction.

So we have progressively expanded our number system by asking for an answer x to the following equations:

- $1 + x = 0 \Rightarrow$ negative numbers

- $2x = 3 \Rightarrow$ fractions

- $x^2 = 2 \Rightarrow$ irrational numbers

- $x^2 = -1 \Rightarrow$ imaginary numbers

You may have been taught that there is no such things as the square root of a negative number. In fact throughout history, people have made such comments against irrational and negative numbers too. A number is a concept, not a thing. Provided the concept is sound, then we can say that the number exists. Bank accounts with a line of credit provides a model of negative numbers, which together with the whole numbers forms the *integers*, denoted $\mathbb{Z}$. Lengths of geometric objects such as triangles and circles provide a model for *real numbers*, which include all rational and irrational numbers. What might be a model of $\sqrt{-1}$?

Imagine extending the real number line into a 2 dimensional number plane. Each point is labelled by a pair of real numbers (x, y), called the point's *coordinate*. To

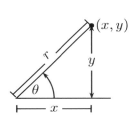

Figure A.2: Polar coordinates. Complex numbers are points on a plane which can be expressed in terms of a distance r from the origin, and angle θ made with the x-axis. Contrast with Cartesian coordinates (x, y).

add two points together, you add each component of the pair:

$$(x_1, y_1) + (x_2, y_2) = (x_1 + x_2, y_1 + y_2) \tag{A.1}$$

This sort of addition is also known as *vector addition*, and illustrated in figure A.3.

Multiplication becomes a combination of scaling (regular multiplication of positive numbers) and rotation. Consider our points expressed in polar coordinates (see Fig A.2), which is the distance of the point from the origin $(0, 0)$, called the *modulus* and the angle made with the real number line, called the *phase*. Then to multiply two numbers, multiply the two moduli together to get a new number, and add the two phase angles:

$$p(r_1, \theta_1) \times p(r_2, \theta_2) = p(r_1 r_2, \theta_1 + \theta_2). \tag{A.2}$$

It is clear that multiplying two positive numbers ($\theta_1 = \theta_2 = 0$) gives the same result as the usual rules for real number multiplication. The same is true when multiplying by negative numbers. A negative number has a phase angle of $180°$, so flips a negative number to a positive and vice-versa. A number having phase angle $90°$ will rotate another $90°$ when squared to give a phase angle of $180°$, so a number with a phase angle of $90°$ is the square root of a negative number. $\sqrt{-1}$ is just the number lying distance one from the origin, at right angles to the real line. Mathematical convention denotes this number by the letter i (for imaginary). Every number in the plane can be written as the sum $x + yi$, and is called a *complex number*.

Converting between polar coordinates $p(r, \theta)$ and Cartesian coordinates (x, y) can be done with a little trigonometry:

$$
\begin{aligned}
x &= r \cos \theta \\
y &= r \sin \theta \\
r &= \sqrt{x^2 + y^2} \\
\theta &= \arctan(y/x)
\end{aligned}
$$

A little bit of mathematical manipulation should convince you that eq (A.2) can also be expressed as:

$$(x_1 + y_1 i) \times (x_2 + y_2 i) = x_1 x_2 - y_1 y_2 + (x_1 y_2 + x_2 y_1)i \quad \text{(A.3)}$$

Speaking of polar coordinates, a very simple way writing $p(r, \theta)$ is

$$p(r, \theta) = r \exp(i\theta) = r e^{i\theta}, \quad \text{(A.4)}$$

where θ is expressed in terms of *radians*, an angular measure such that $180° = \pi \approx 3.1415926\ldots$ radians The proof of this formula takes us beyond the scope of this appendix, but is not too difficult. Carl Friedrich Gauss, 19th Century's most preeminent mathematician discovered this formula, and was struck by the beauty of the special case $p(1, \pi)$:

$$e^{i\pi} + 1 = 0. \quad \text{(A.5)}$$

This equation connects 5 of the most important numbers $(e, i, \pi, 1, 0)$ in mathematics in a single equation involving no other terms!

You can also learn more about complex numbers through the Wikibook High School Mathematics Extension[2].

The next question you will probably have is whether the concept of number can be extended to higher dimensions. Is there such a thing as a number "volume", for example? The answer depends on what you mean by number. Mathematicians define things by writing down rules called *axioms* that mathematical objects need to obey. A very important property is for numbers to commute, that it doesn't matter which order you multiply two numbers together, you will always get the same answer, ie $xy = yx$. It turns out that rotations in higher dimensions do not commute, a fact that can be confirmed by picking up a book and rotating it about two different axes. The resulting orientation of the book will depend on the order in which you performed the rotations.

However, if you are prepared to relax the commutivity requirement of multiplication, then there are number-like systems in 4 dimensions (called *quaternions*) and 8 dimensions (called *octonians*). These non-commutative division algebras have not one but two possible answers to $c = a/b$, depending on whether $bc = a$ or $cb = a$.

In physics and engineering, however, there is little interest in using quaternions and other like systems. Vector theory allows one to describe objects of arbitrary dimensionality, a subject we will turn to next.

Mathematically speaking, we say that addition forms an *Abelian group*, ie it obeys commutivity, associativity, the presence of an identity element (0), and a unique

---

[2] http://en.wikibooks.org/wiki/HSE_Complex_number

inverse for each element $(-x)$. If a set of objects also has multiplication between the objects, and multiplication also forms an Abelian group (with identity 1 and inverse $1/x, x \neq 0$), then we say the set of objects is a *field*. Fields capture the essence of what we mean by "number", and are an important concept for vector spaces. Complex numbers constitute the most general notion of field possible.

Finally a bit of useful notation for referring to the set of all (infinitely many) whole numbers, all integers and so on:

1. the set of all whole numbers is denoted $\mathbb{N}$.

2. the set of all integers is denoted $\mathbb{Z}$.

3. the set of all rational numbers is denoted $\mathbb{Q}$.

4. the set of all real numbers is denoted $\mathbb{R}$.

5. the set of all complex numbers is denoted $\mathbb{C}$.

In short, wherever you see a "blackboard" style symbol like these, it means the set of all numbers of a particular class.

A.3   Vector Spaces

In high school, vectors are often introduced as part of physics. They are quantities that have both magnitude and a direction. *Velocity*, for example is a vector having *speed* as magnitude, and pointing in the direction of travel. Vectors can be added to each other, and scaled by a number (an element of a field to be more precise). Fig A.3 shows how the resultant vector is obtained from adding two vectors together in 2 dimensions. Scaling a

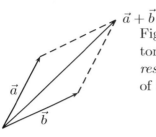

$\vec{a} + \vec{b}$

Figure A.3: Addition of two vectors is another vector (called the *resultant*) formed by the diagonal of the parallelogram

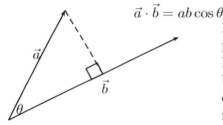

$\vec{a} \cdot \vec{b} = ab \cos \theta$

Figure A.4: The inner product multiplies the length of one vector, by the *projection* of the other vector onto the first.

vector by a positive number merely lengthens the vector, and scaling by a negative number flips the vector around to point the other way.

A *vector space* is a set of vectors so that all combinations of additions and scalings of set members are also members of the vector space.

We humans, living in a 3 dimensional world, have little difficulty in imagining 2 dimensional and 3 dimensional vectors. But higher dimensions take some getting used to. Vectors can be written as a list of coordinates, which are the projections of the vector onto a standard basis set of vectors, for example the x-axis, y-axis and so on. Obviously it is not hard to imagine what a list of 10 numbers looks like. But that is just a 10 dimensional vector! Because there are n real or complex numbers, these spaces are denoted $\mathbb{R}^n$ or $\mathbb{C}^n$ respectively.

We can add two vectors to get another vector, and

multiply a scalar by a vector to get another vector, but in general, multiplication of two vectors to make another vector doesn't make sense. However, for most vector spaces we're interested in here, it is possible to multiply two vectors to get a real number. This is called an *inner product*[3]. For real vectors $x \in \mathbb{R}^n$, this is defined by:

$$\vec{x} \cdot \vec{y} = \sum_i x_i y_i, \tag{A.6}$$

where $\sum$ refers to the sum of a sequence (see §A.5)

For complex vectors, the inner product formula is slightly different:

$$\vec{x} \cdot \vec{y} = \sum_i x_i^* y_i \tag{A.7}$$

where * refers to complex conjugation, or replacing the imaginary component of a number by its negative:

$$(x + iy)^* = x - iy, \quad x, y \in \mathbb{R} \tag{A.8}$$

Of extreme importance in vector space theory, is the notion of a *linear* function. A linear function is a function f that satisfies a very simple rule:

$$f(a\vec{x} + b\vec{y}) = af(\vec{x}) + bf(\vec{y}) \tag{A.9}$$

where a and b are elements of the field ($\mathbb{R}$ or $\mathbb{C}$), and $\vec{x}$ and $\vec{y}$ are vectors. f may be a scalar function (ie return a number) or it may be a vector valued function.

An example of a linear function is given by the inner product (see Fig A.4). Fixing the vector $\vec{y}$, and allowing $\vec{x}$

---

[3]There is also an outer product, an exterior product, a cross product (effectively a specialised exterior product for 3 dimensions) and a tensor product.

to vary, you can readily see how the function $f_{\vec{y}}(\vec{x}) = \vec{x} \cdot \vec{y}$ is linear.

Linear functions are also often called *linear operators*, and are used to represent *observables* in quantum mechanics. If the dimensionality of the vector space is finite, then linear operators may be represented by a *matrix*, which is an array of numbers $F_{ij} = \hat{e}_i \cdot f(\hat{e}_j)$, where $\hat{e}_i$ is the i-th basis vector $(0, 0, ...1, 0...0)$, where the 1 appears in the i-th place.

Matrices (and linear operators) themselves can be added and scaled, so form their own vector space, of dimension $m \times n$. Further more, the operation of composing two linear operators is a form of non-commutative multiplication, and is called *matrix multiplication*:

$$(FG)_{ij} = \hat{e}_i \cdot f(g(\hat{e}_j)) \qquad (A.10)$$

$$(FG)_{ij} = \sum_k F_{ik} G_{kj}$$

$$(A.11)$$

A.3.1 Hermitian and Unitary operators

The adjoint of an operator A is defined in terms of the inner product, ie

$$A^\dagger \vec{x} \cdot \vec{y} \equiv \vec{x} \cdot A\vec{y}, \qquad (A.12)$$

for all vectors $\vec{x}$ and $\vec{y}$.

In matrix representation, the components of $A^\dagger$ are found by transposing the matrix, and taking the complex conjugate :

$$a^\dagger_{ij} = a^*_{ji}. \qquad (A.13)$$

A *Hermitian* operator is self-adjoint, ie $A^\dagger = A$. Hermitian operators always have real eigenvalues, and oper-

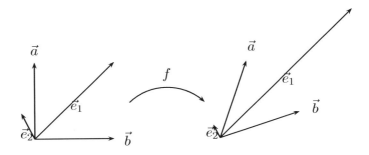

Figure A.5: Diagram showing how linear maps rotate, stretch and squash vectors. Vectors that just stretch or squash without rotation are known as *eigenvectors* (eg $\vec{e}_1, \vec{e}_2$ above), and the amount they are scaled by is called an *eigenvalue*.

ators with only real eigenvalues are always Hermitian, so physical observables are always Hermitian.

A *Unitary* operator has its adjoint equal to its inverse:

$$U^\dagger U = I, \qquad (A.14)$$

where I is the identity operator. Unitary operators are a generalisation of the numbers $e^{i\theta}$, just as Hermitian operators are a generalisation of real numbers. Interestingly, every unitary operator can be written as $U = \exp(iH)$, where H is Hermitian.

A.3.2 Eigenvalues and Eigenvectors

Every linear operator has certain directions which remain unchanged upon application of the operator:

$$A\vec{v}_i = \lambda_i \vec{v}_i. \qquad (A.15)$$

Any such vector $\vec{v}_i$ is called an *eigenvector*, and the associated value λ_i is called an eigenvalue. Eigenvalues represent the possible outcomes of measurements in quantum mechanics.

A.4   Sets

More basic than numbers or vectors are *sets*. A simple understanding of sets is that they are collections of distinct objects, called *elements* or *members*. The set members may be anything — eg a set of distinctly-shaped pebbles, but more usually they are of mathematical objects. We have already met some sets — the set of whole numbers $\mathbb{N}$, or the set of n-dimensional vectors $\mathbb{R}^n$ for example.

We write "x is an element of the set S" using the notation $x \in S$. Thus $x \in \mathbb{R}$ means x is a real number.

We also talk about subsets, which contain some of the elements of a set. The set $S = \{0, 1, 2, 3, 4, 5, 6, 7, 8, 9\}$ is a subset of the set of whole numbers, which we write $S \subset \mathbb{N}$ (or equivalently $\mathbb{N} \supset S$, i.e. $\mathbb{N}$ *contains S*). Every set contains itself as a subset, as well as the empty set which contains no elements at all (denoted $\emptyset$).

When talking about the subsets of a specific set U, we can form the complement of a set $A \subset U$ as

$$\bar{A} \equiv \{x \in U \,|\, x \notin A\}. \tag{A.16}$$

The set U is sometimes called a *universal set*, if we are discussing set theory divorced of a particular application. Obviously $U = \bar{\emptyset}$.

The number of elements in a set, or *cardinality* is written as the set sandwiched between two vertical bars. So

$$
\begin{aligned}
|S| &= 10 \\
|\emptyset| &= 0
\end{aligned}
$$

Sets may be combined using the operations of *union* (written ∪) and *intersection* (written ∩). The intersection of two sets is the set of elements appearing in both sets. The union of two sets contains all elements in both sets, with duplicates removed. This leads us to one of the first simple theorems of set theory:

$$|A \cup B| = |A| + |B| - |A \cap B| \qquad \text{(A.17)}$$

This satisfies the important additivity axiom of a measure (see eq (4.1)).

A.4.1 Infinite Cardinality

The behaviour of finite sets are quite simple, and were used as part of my education of basic arithmetic in primary school. I appreciate that using set theory to teach basic arithmetic is a fashion that comes and goes, so not everyone will have this grounding.

However, when sets have an infinite number of elements, our familiar intuition tends to fail us. For example, it might seem that there are twice as many whole numbers as even numbers, as after all, every odd number is left out. However, to compare cardinality between two sets, we must arrange a one to one correspondence between elements of the set. If this can be done, the two sets have the same cardinality. With even numbers, every even number j corresponds to whole number i by the relation $j = 2i$, and every whole number i, corresponds to an even number $2i$.

There are an infinite number of whole numbers, so should we just write $|\mathbb{N}| = \infty$? Unfortunately, it turns out that not all infinite sets have the same cardinality, so there are many different types of infinity (in fact an infinite number of them). The smallest infinity is the cardinality of the natural numbers, $|\mathbb{N}| = \aleph_0$, pronounced "aleph null", aleph being the first letter of the Hebrew alphabet. The next largest cardinal number is called $\aleph_1$ and so on.

You should find it a simple exercise to show that $|\mathbb{Z}| = \aleph_0$ and $|\mathbb{Q}| = \aleph_0$. For the latter exercise, if $m/n \geq 1$ for $m, n \in \mathbb{N}$, let $i = 2(\sum_{j=1}^{n} j + m)$. If $m/n < 1$ use the formula $i = 2(\sum_{j=1}^{m} j + n) + 1$. This maps the positive rationals to the positive integers, and by changing signs the negative rationals to the negative integers. This shows that there are at least as many integers as rational numbers. Since the integers are contained within the rationals, there must be exactly as many rationals as integers.

Georg Cantor was the first to investigate infinite sets in the 19th century. He invented the *diagonalisation argument* demonstrating that there are more real numbers than integers. This argument has been applied in many different situations, being used by Alan Turing for example to demonstrate that no general algorithm exists to solve the Halting problem. Bruno Marchal relies upon diagonalisation in his universal dovetailer argument[89], so it is worthwhile describing it here as the idea is quite simple, and very powerful.

Firstly let us assume that the cardinality of the reals is $\aleph_0$, and attempt to derive a contradiction. If $|\mathbb{R}| = \aleph_0$, then we can write the real numbers in a list, indexed by the whole number that it is mapped to. The list might look something like figure A.6:

We can construct a new real number by selecting its ith decimal place as a different digit from the ith decimal of the ith number in the list (eg by adding one to it). If this new number were a member of the list, the jth number, say, then we have a contradiction, because the newly constructed number differs from the jth number of

0.6123993128589185...
0.1231238898582104...
0.1285578531083894...
0.1523741287312784...
0.2349583228908132...
0.1271329632793247...
0.1239732628012384...
0.1238923732904812...
0.1209861326743838...
0.0984378270283483...
0.9822600948190348...
0.1328345734932890...
0.2685473688547732...
0.0348765639379573...
0.3275638299370836...
0.6452774902705720...

Figure A.6: Cantor's diagonalisation argument. The number 0.7394633831248641... (for example) cannot be on the list.

the list in the jth decimal place. So it cannot be found on the list.

So there must be more real numbers than integers. Conventionally, the cardinality of the reals is denoted $c = |\mathbb{R}|$ (c for continuum). It is actually undecidable according to the usual number theory axioms whether there are any infinities in between $\aleph_0$ and c. The statement that c is the next infinity greater than $\aleph_0$ (ie $c = \aleph_1$) is known as the *continuum hypothesis*. One can consistently believe in the hypothesis, or not, and still end up with the same rules of finite mathematics. Differences appear in the infinite.

The number of infinite length bitstrings is $2^{\aleph_0}$ since the number of finite length bitstrings of length n is 2^n. $2^{\aleph_0} = c$, as each bitstring can be considered to be the binary expansion of a real number on the interval $[0, 1]$. Note that two bitstrings map to the same rational number in certain cases, for example $1000...$ and $0111...$ both match the rational number 0.5, but since there are only

$\aleph_0$ of these, the cardinality of the set of bitstrings is still c.

A.4.2 Measure

As we saw in the previous section, cardinality of finite sets is a measure (§4.5). For line segments $[a, b] \subset \mathbb{R}$, we can define a measure proportional to the length $b - a$ of the segment.

When a cardinality of a subset B of an infinite set A is smaller than $|A|$, we say that B is of *measure zero* with respect to A. So all finite sets of points form a set of measure zero in $\mathbb{R}$, as does the set of integers. So does the set of rational numbers $\mathbb{Q}$. This latter concept seems a little strange, as any real number can be arbitrarily approximated by a rational number, yet the rationals are sufficiently sparse they contribute nothing to the measure of a set of reals.

Whilst on the topic of zero measure sets, the Cantor set (see Fig. 4.1) is also a set of measure zero, as are any *fractals* with Hausdorf dimension less than the embedding dimension. Don't worry, you don't need to know this to understand this book!

A.5 Summation and difference — Calculus

In mathematical formulae, it is convenient to denote the sum of a series as:

$$\sum_{i=1}^{n} x_i = x_1 + x_2 + \ldots x_n \qquad (A.18)$$

The lower index of the $\sum$ sign indicates the index (i) and the lower bound of the sequence. The upper bound is

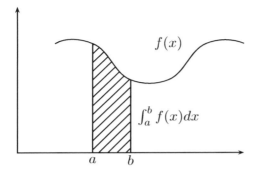

Figure A.7: An integral is the area under a curve between two limits

written above the $\sum$ sign. If the limits are obvious, then they're often left out.

Differences are usually indicated by another Greek letter:

$$\Delta x_i = x_{i+1} - x_i \tag{A.19}$$

Using this notation, we can write an approximation for the area under a curve $f(x)$ (see fig A.7)

$$A \approx \sum_{i=0}^{n} f(x_i)\Delta x_i, \tag{A.20}$$

$$x_i = a + i\Delta x_i, \quad x_n = b \tag{A.21}$$

This approximation will become more and more accurate (provided $f(x)$ is sufficiently well behaved) as more and more points are added. To indicate the limit as $n \to \infty$, we write:

$$A = \lim_{n \to \infty} \sum_{i=0}^{n} f(x_i)\Delta x_i = \int_a^b f(x)dx \tag{A.22}$$

where the replacement $\sum \to \int$ and $\Delta \to d$ indicates that a limiting process has taken place.

Congratulations — you have just understood the subject *integral calculus*. *Differential calculus* can be approached similarly, where the interest is computing the

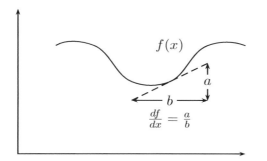

Figure A.8: A derivative is the slope of a curve at a point

slope of some curve $f(x)$ (see Fig. A.8). We approximate the slope by dividing the change in the function by the interval we're measuring it over:

$$s(x) \approx \frac{f(x + \Delta x) - f(x)}{\Delta x} = \frac{\Delta f(x)}{\Delta x} \quad \text{(A.23)}$$

$$s(x) = \lim_{\Delta x \to 0} \frac{\Delta f}{\Delta x} = \frac{df}{dx} \quad \text{(A.24)}$$

The connection between integral and differential calculus can be most easily seen by considering the case where $f(t)$ is the speed of your car at time t. The distance you have travelled since you started your journey at time $t = 0$ is given by $d(t) = \int_0^t f(s)ds$, and the acceleration of your car at the instant t is given by $\frac{df}{dt}$.

Whilst calculus can get quite involved technically, the above description suffices for the purpose of this book. You will occasionally see some other notations used for different concepts. For a function of more than one variable ($f(x, y)$ say), the notation $\frac{\partial f}{\partial x}$ means take the derivative of f holding all of the other variables fixed. The reason for different notation from $\frac{df}{dx}$ is that the other variables may well depend on x as well, so in general $\frac{df}{dx}$ (called the *total* derivate) is not the same as the *partial derivative* $\frac{\partial f}{\partial x}$.

With scalar functions of vector arguments, the derivative is often written ∇f.

Appendix B

How Soon until Doom?

Curiously, in spite of all the sophisticated Bayesian analyses of the Doomsday Argument, there have been very few published calculations on just how soon the doomsday might occur. Bostrom mentions a figure of 1200 years with 75% probability[20], but this is assuming that population levels stabilise at say 12 billion.

One counter-argument to the Doomsday Argument argues that the DA applies equally to ancient Greeks or Romans, yet clearly our species has survived and even prospered dramatically since then. In this appendix, I present a calculation of the expected time to doomsday, assuming a worst case scenario of exponential population growth from now until doomsday.

Let N denote the total number of humans who ever live, and C, the number who have been born to date. Let $x = C/N \in [0,1]$ be fraction of human "birth history" that has already passed. Then assuming that the birth rate increases exponentially with time constant r, we have:

$$\int_0^\tau b e^{rt} dt = N(1-x) = C\frac{(1-x)}{x} \tag{B.1}$$

where b is the current birth rate, and τ is the time until doomsday.

Rearranging equation (B.1), we obtain

$$\tau = \frac{1}{r}\left[\ln(\alpha(1-x)+x) - \ln x\right] \tag{B.2}$$

where we have defined the dimensionless parameter $\alpha = rC/b$ for convenience.

The self-sampling assumption assumes we are equally likely to be born as any individual in history, consequently x is drawn from a uniform distribution on $[0,1]$. The expected value of τ, or the time to doomsday, is given by integrating equation (B.2) over x:

$$\begin{aligned} \langle \tau \rangle &= \frac{1}{r}\int_0^1 \left[\ln(\alpha(1-x)+x) - \ln x\right] dx \\ &= \frac{\alpha \ln \alpha}{r(\alpha - 1)}. \end{aligned} \tag{B.3}$$

Now we need to determine the values r and α for historical periods of interest. We do not have historical birth rates, but it is reasonable to assume that the birthrate b is proportional to the population size $P(t)$ at that time, with a constant of proportionality that hasn't varied much, except in the last quarter century when the impact of widely available effective birth control reduces this constant of proportionality.

The total number of humans born is just the integral of the birthrate, ie $C = \int_{-\infty}^{\text{now}} b(t)dt$, so we don't need the absolute value of this constant of proportionality in order to compute α.

Year	Pop	Year	Pop	Year	Pop	Year	Pop
-10000	1	1	170	1250	400	1900	1550
-8000	5	200	190	1300	360	1910	1750
-6500	5	400	190	1340	443	1920	1860
-5000	5	500	190	1400	350	1930	2070
-4000	7	600	200	1500	425	1940	2300
-3000	14	700	207	1600	545	1950	2400
-2000	27	800	220	1650	470	1960	3020
-1000	50	900	226	1700	600	1970	3700
-500	100	1000	254	1750	629	1980	4400
-400	162	1100	301	1800	813	1990	5270
-200	150	1200	360	1850	1128	2000	6060

Table B.1: Population data extracted from [141, 139]. Years are given in terms of Common Era (also known as AD). Negative values refer to BCE dates. Population values are expressed in millions. This dataset is plotted in figure 5.2.

The data I use here is listed in table B.1. One tricky parameter to estimate is the number of humans that lived prior to 10,000 BCE — my estimate is that it would be no more than one billion (10^9), assuming a population size significantly less than a million over a period of 100,000 years, and an annual birthrate of 4 children per hundred individuals ($0.04P$).

The population growth rate r can be deduced from:

$$\begin{aligned} P(t + \Delta t) &= P(t)e^{r\Delta t} \\ r &= \frac{1}{\Delta t}\ln\frac{P(t+\Delta t)}{P(t)}. \end{aligned} \tag{B.4}$$

So now α can be deduced from

$$\alpha = r\frac{\int_{-10000}^{t}P(t)dt + 2.5\times 10^{10}}{P(t)} \tag{B.5}$$

The results are shown in table B.2. Throughout most of recorded history, the doomsday is sufficiently far off not to concern the people of the time (even if they knew the Doomsday Argument). The ancient Greeks would have predicted doom around the time of Christ, but clearly various dark ages, wars and epidemics intervened to constrain human population growth, and so postpone doomsday. Only in the 20th century, does the doomsday loom sufficiently close to be of concern to our grandchildren. Clearly, the scenario postulated here of a spectacular population crash following a period of exponential growth is overly pessimistic. In reality, population growth is likely to slow, and then go in reverse, as it did during the Middle Ages, which could postpone doomsday by a millennia or so.

Year	r	α	$\langle\tau\rangle$	Year	r	α	$\langle\tau\rangle$
-1000	0.0006	1.82	2159	1500	0.0019	3.05	855
-500	0.0013	2.74	1145	1600	0.0024	3.30	689
-400	0.0048	6.37	455	1650	-0.0029	-4.70	
-200	-0.0003	-0.62		1700	0.0048	6.32	448
1	0.0006	1.01	1621	1750	0.0009	1.21	1165
200	0.0005	0.93	1725	1800	0.0051	5.36	402
400	0.0000	0.00		1850	0.0065	5.25	312
500	0.0000	0.00		1900	0.0063	4.03	291
600	0.0005	1.00	1957	1910	0.0121	6.93	186
700	0.0003	0.68	2396	1920	0.0060	3.34	282
800	0.0006	1.20	1800	1930	0.0106	5.37	193
900	0.0002	0.54	2704	1940	0.0105	4.86	189
1000	0.0011	2.22	1243	1950	0.0042	1.92	320
1100	0.0016	2.89	957	1960	0.0229	8.50	105
1200	0.0017	2.73	886	1970	0.0203	6.33	107
1250	0.0021	3.00	782	1980	0.0173	4.71	113
1300	-0.0021	-3.44		1990	0.0180	4.28	105
1340	0.0051	7.09	439	2000	0.0139	3.02	118
1400	-0.0039	-7.03					

Table B.2: Results for population growth r, α and expected time to doomsday ($\langle\tau\rangle$) for population data.

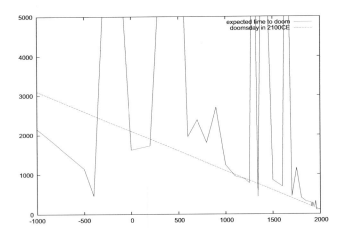

Figure B.1: Plot of expected time to doom from 1000BCE to present. Only in the twentieth century does the expected time drop below 300 years, and is currently around 100 years. Only during the Greek golden age (500BCE-400BCE) was the predicted time substantially earlier than 2100 CE (dashed line).

Appendix C

Anthropic selection from arbitrary measures

In most discussions of anthropic selection in the literature, (see eg Bostrom[20]), it is assumed that only a finite set of possibilities are selected from ($i = 0 \ldots n$), and that each of these has a definite probability P_i of being selected. The most likely outcome is then taken to be the outcome having the greatest probability of being selected, or if more than one outcome has the maximum probability, a random selection of those — i.e. $i : P_i \geq P_j \forall j$. Clearly this procedure also works for a countably infinite number of possibilities also, with $\sum_i P_i = 1$.

It is clear that this principle can be easily extended to a continuum of cases if a probability distribution $P(x)$ is given — given an $\epsilon > 0$, discretise the continuum into segments $x_i \leq x < x_{i+1}$. Then this case converts to the previous example, with $P_i = \int_{x_i}^{x_{i+1}} P(x) dx$. An example is given in the top half of figure 5.1.

What happens if our measure is more general than a

probability distribution? Consider the lower half of figure 5.1, where we have an unnormalisable positive measure. Informally, the answer seems clear — we should select a random outcome from the set with most measure, ie something like the rectangle marked B in the graph. To formalise this, let $\mu : U \to [0, \infty]$ be the measure, and take an infinite sequence of finite measure sets $U_i \subset U$, such that

$$U_i \supseteq U_{i-1} \text{and} \int_{U_i} \mu(x)dx < \infty \qquad (C.1)$$

Now choose an $\epsilon > 0$, and use this to discretise the y axis of graph of $\mu(x)$ into segments $\mu_j \leq \mu(x) < \mu_{j+1}$. The ratio

$$\rho_i(\mu_j) = \frac{\int_{\{x:x\in U_i \text{and} |\mu(x)-\mu_j|<\epsilon\}} \mu(x)dx}{\int_{U_i} \mu(x)dx} \in [0, 1]. \qquad (C.2)$$

Suppose this sequence converges for $i \to \infty$ (as it does for the case illustrated in figure 5.1. Then $P_j = \lim_{i\to\infty} \rho_i(\mu_j)$ forms a discrete probability distribution, and we may select the μ_j (or perhaps several) that have greatest probability, then select x at random from the set $\{x : |\mu(x) - \mu_j| < \epsilon\}$. In our figure 5.1 example, $\rho_i(\mu)$ converges rapidly to a Kronecker delta ($P_j = \delta_{jk}, \mu_k = \max(\mu)$),

Equation (C.2) can be generalised to the complex measure case $\mu(x) \in \mathbb{C}$. If the measure is sufficiently symmetric such for each set A, another set A^* exists with measure $\mu(A^*) = \mu(A)^*$, and also for subsets:

$$\forall X \subset A, \exists X^* \in A^* : \mu(X^*) = \mu(X)^*, \qquad (C.3)$$

then we can choose the sets U_i so that the integrals in eq (C.2) are real valued:

$$\rho_i(\mu_j) = \frac{\int_{\{x:x\in U_i \text{and} ||\mu(x)|-\mu_j|<\epsilon\}} \mu(x)dx}{\int_{U_i} \mu(x)dx} \in [0, 1]. \qquad (C.4)$$

The most general measure is a *spectral measure*, with $\mu(x) \in B$, for some Banach space B. We can generalise formula (C.2) to this case by selecting a direction vector $\vec{b} \in B$ such that

$$\forall A \subset \mathrm{dom}(\mu), \exists A^* \subset \mathrm{dom}(\mu) : \mu(A) + \mu(A^*) \quad \propto \quad \vec{b}$$
$$\forall X \subset A, \exists X^* \subset A^* : \mu(X) + \mu(X^*) \quad \propto \quad \vec{b}$$

Then we can write

$$\rho_i(\mu_j) \int_{\{x : x \in U_i \mathrm{and} ||\mu(x)| - \mu_j| < \epsilon\}} \mu(x) dx = \int_{U_i} \mu(x) dx. \tag{C.5}$$

Appendix D

Derivation of Quantum Postulates 1–3

In §7.1, I argue that knowledge about the world is constructed in an evolutionary approach. Observer moments $\psi(t)$ are sets of possibilities consistent with what is known at that point in time, providing variation upon which anthropic selection acts. The PROJECTION postulate says that an observer is free to choose an observable A, which divides the observer moment $\psi \in V$ into a discrete set of outcomes $\{\psi_a : a \in \mathbb{N}\}$. We wish to determine the probability $P_\psi(\psi_a)$ of outcome a being observed. In order to do this, we need to employ the Kolmogorov probability axioms[81]:

(A1) If A and B are events, then so is the *intersection* $A \cap B$, the *union* $A \cup B$ and the *difference* $A - B$.

(A2) The *sample space* S is an event, called the *certain event*, and the *empty set* $\emptyset$ is an event, called the *impossible* event.

(A3) To each event E, $P(E) \in [0,1]$ denotes the *probability* of that event.

(A4) $P(S) = 1$.

(A5) If $A \cap B = \emptyset$, then $P(A \cup B) = P(A) + P(B)$.

(A6) For a decreasing sequence $A_1 \supset A_2 \supset \cdots \supset A_n \cdots$ of events with $\bigcap_n A_n = \emptyset$, we have $\lim_{n \to \infty} P(A_n) = 0$.

Where the axioms refer to events, we shall read outcome, or observation.

Consider now the projection operator $\mathcal{P}_{\{a\}} : V \longrightarrow V$, acting on a ensemble $\psi \in V$, V being the set of all such ensembles, to produce $\psi_a = \mathcal{P}_{\{a\}}\psi$, where $a \in S$ is an outcome of an observation. We have not at this stage assumed that $\mathcal{P}_{\{a\}}$ is linear. Define addition for two distinct outcomes $a \neq b$ as follows:

$$\mathcal{P}_{\{a\}}\psi + \mathcal{P}_{\{b\}}\psi = \mathcal{P}_{\{a,b\}}\psi, \tag{D.1}$$

from which it follows that

$$\mathcal{P}_{A \subset S}\psi = \sum_{a \in A} \mathcal{P}_{\{a\}}\psi \tag{D.2}$$

$$\mathcal{P}_{A \cup B}\psi = \mathcal{P}_A\psi + \mathcal{P}_B\psi - \mathcal{P}_{A \cap B}\psi \tag{D.3}$$

$$\mathcal{P}_{A \cap B}\psi = \mathcal{P}_A\mathcal{P}_B\psi = \mathcal{P}_B\mathcal{P}_A\psi. \tag{D.4}$$

These results extend to continuous sets by replacing the discrete sums by integration over the sets with uniform measure. However it should be noted that no real measurement discriminates arbitrarily finely, in practice all measurements will return values from a discrete set (gradations on a meter, numbers on a digital display, and so on). However quantum theory will often reason as though measurements form a continuum, for computational convenience.

Let the ensemble $\psi \in U \equiv \{\mathcal{P}_A\psi | A \subset S\}$ be a "reference state", corresponding to the certain event. It encodes information about the whole ensemble. Denote the probability of a set of outcomes $A \subset S$ by $P_\psi(\mathcal{P}_A\psi)$. Clearly

$$P_\psi(\mathcal{P}_S\psi) = P_\psi(\psi) = 1 \qquad (D.5)$$

by virtue of (A4). Also, by virtue of Eq. (D.3) and (A4),

$$P_\psi((\mathcal{P}_A + \mathcal{P}_B)\psi) = P_\psi(\mathcal{P}_A\psi) + P_\psi(\mathcal{P}_B\psi) \quad \text{if } A \cap B = \emptyset. \qquad (D.6)$$

Eq (D.6) pertains to the situation of a single observer partitioning observation space into disjoint sets. However, observer moments have multiple observers observing them — if this were a natural number $a \in \mathbb{N}$ say, we can interpret the formula $P_\psi(a\mathcal{P}_A\psi) = aP_\psi(\mathcal{P}_A\psi)$ as the *measure* of observer moment ψ_A given that a observers are observing ψ being partitioned into ψ_A and $\psi_{\bar{A}}$. Continuing along these lines, if a observers were partitioning ψ into ψ_A and $\psi_{\bar{A}}$, and b observers were partitioning ψ into ψ_B and $\psi_{\bar{B}}$ respectively, then

$$P_\psi((a\mathcal{P}_A + b\mathcal{P}_B)\psi) = aP_\psi(\mathcal{P}_A\psi) + bP_\psi(\mathcal{P}_B\psi) \qquad (D.7)$$

is the measure of the combined observer moment $a\psi_A + b\psi_B$.

In §4.5, I argue that in general the observer moment measure can be complex, so indeed the a and b in equation (D.7) must also be complex numbers in general. More general division algebras such as quaternions or octonians cannot support equations of the form (D.7) without ambiguity. Thus V, the set of all observer moments, is a vector space over the complex numbers.

The probability function P can be used to define an inner product as follows. Our reference state ψ can be expressed as a sum over the projected states

$$\psi = \sum_{a \in S} \mathcal{P}_{\{a\}} \psi \equiv \sum_{a \in S} \psi_a. \qquad \text{(D.8)}$$

Let $V = \mathcal{L}(\psi_a) \supset U$ be the linear span of this basis set. Then, $\forall \phi, \xi \in V$, such that $\phi = \sum_{a \in S} \phi_a \psi_a$ and $\xi = \sum_{a \in S} \xi_a \psi_a$, the inner product $\langle \phi, \xi \rangle$ is defined by

$$\langle \phi, \xi \rangle = \sum_{a \in S} \phi_a^* \xi_a P_\psi(\psi_a). \qquad \text{(D.9)}$$

It is straightforward to show that this definition has the usual properties of an inner product, and that ψ is normalized ($\langle \psi, \psi \rangle = 1$). The probabilities $P_\psi(\psi_a)$ are given by

$$
\begin{aligned}
P_\psi(\psi_a) &= \langle \psi_a, \psi_a \rangle \\
&= \langle \psi, \mathcal{P}_a \psi \rangle \\
&= |\langle \psi, \hat{\psi}_a \rangle|^2,
\end{aligned} \qquad \text{(D.10)}
$$

where $\hat{\psi}_a = \psi_a / \sqrt{P_\psi(\psi_a)}$ is normalised.

Thus we have derived the third quantum mechanical postulate, Born's formula (7.2). We have established that V is an inner product space, we still need to demonstrate its completeness, for which we need axiom (A6).

Consider a sequence of sets of outcomes $A_0 \supset A_1 \ldots$, and denote by $A \subset A_n \forall n$ the unique maximal subset (possibly empty), such that $\bar{A} \bigcap_n A_n = \emptyset$. Then the difference $\mathcal{P}_{A_i} - \mathcal{P}_A$ is well defined, and so

$$
\begin{aligned}
\langle (\mathcal{P}_{A_i} - \mathcal{P}_A)\psi, (\mathcal{P}_{A_i} - \mathcal{P}_A)\psi \rangle &= P_\psi((\mathcal{P}_{A_i} - \mathcal{P}_A)\psi) \\
&= P_\psi((\mathcal{P}_{A_i} + \mathcal{P}_{\bar{A}} - \mathcal{P}_S)\psi) \\
&= P_\psi(\mathcal{P}_{A_i \cap \bar{A}}). \qquad \text{(D.11)}
\end{aligned}
$$

By axiom (A6),

$$\lim_{n\to\infty} \langle (\mathcal{P}_{A_i} - \mathcal{P}_A)\psi, (\mathcal{P}_{A_i} - \mathcal{P}_A)\psi \rangle = 0, \qquad (D.12)$$

so $\mathcal{P}_{A_i}\psi$ is a Cauchy sequence that converges to $\mathcal{P}_A\psi \in U$. Hence U is complete under the inner product (D.9). It follows that V is complete also, and is therefore a *Hilbert* space, justifying the first quantum mechanical postulate.

Finally for the second postulate, we need Lewontin's heritability requirement. In between observations, the observer moment may evolve provided information is conserved. We require that $\psi(t')$ can be computed deterministically from $\psi(t)$, for $t' > t$. This can only be true if $\psi(t)$ is analytic at t. The most general equation for computing ψ as a function of time is a first order differential equation:

$$\frac{d\psi}{dt} = \mathcal{H}(\psi). \qquad (D.13)$$

$\mathcal{H}$ does not depend on time, as in this picture time is purely a first person phenomenon. We can say that equation D.13 provides a clock by which an observer can measure a time interval between two observations. Since measurement of time is given by the clock, we adopt the convention that the clock is constant process.

Since we suppose that ψ_a is also a solution of Eq. D.13 (ie that the act of observation does not change the physics of the system), $\mathcal{H}$ must be linear. The certain event must have probability of 1 at all times, so

$$
\begin{aligned}
0 &= \frac{dP_{\psi(t)}(\psi(t))}{dt} \\
&= d/dt \langle \psi, \psi \rangle \\
&= \langle \psi, \mathcal{H}\psi \rangle + \langle \mathcal{H}\psi, \psi \rangle \\
\mathcal{H}^\dagger &= -\mathcal{H}, \qquad (D.14)
\end{aligned}
$$

i.e. $\mathcal{H}$ is i times a Hermitian operator. We may write $\mathcal{H} = \frac{H}{i\hbar}$, and substituting this into eq (D.13) gives us

$$i\hbar\frac{d\psi}{dt} = H\psi, \qquad (\text{D}.15)$$

which is postulate 2, Schrödinger's equation.

Bibliography

In this bibliography, I frequently refer to postings to the
Everything list. Originally, each posting had an explicit
message number which identified the posting within the
archive, but during the writing of this book the archive
was moved to Google groups, and the message number-
ing lost. To find the appropriate message, search on the
posting title given in this bibliography, whichy will get
you the thread (sequence of postings on the same topic)

The Everything list archive can be found at

http://groups.google.com/group/everything-list

and also a partial copy at

http://www.mail-archive.com/everything-
list@eskimo.com/

.

I also refer, where possible to the arXiv identifier of
papers lodged at http://arXiv.org.

Also many other papers appear on personal websites.
It is often useful to perform a web search on the paper's
title.

[1] Chris Adami. *Introduction to Artificial Life.* Springer, 1998.

[2] Chris Adami and N.J.Cerf. Physical complexity of symbolic sequences. *Physica D*, 137:62–69, 2000. arXiv:nlin.AO/9605002.

[3] Chris Adami, Charles Ofria, and Travis Collier. Evolution of biological complexity. *Proc. Natl. Acad. Sci. USA*, 97:4463–4468, 2000.

[4] Robert Adler. Are we on our way back to the dark ages? *New Scientist*, 2506:26–27, 2005.

[5] Philip W. Anderson. More is different. *Science*, 177:393–396, 1972.

[6] Alain Aspect, Phillipe Grangier, and Gérard Roger. Experimental realization of Einstein-Podolsky-Rosen gedankenexperiment; a new violation of Bell's inequalities. *Phys. Rev. Lett.*, 49:91, 1982.

[7] St. Augustine. *Confessions.* 400. http://ccat.sas.upenn.edu/jod/Englishconfessions.html

[8] Per Bak. *How Nature Works.* Oxford UP, Oxford, 1997.

[9] John D. Barrow. *Book of Nothing.* Pantheon, 2001.

[10] John D. Barrow. Glitch! *New Scientist*, 2398:44, 2003. 7th June.

[11] John D. Barrow and Frank J. Tipler. *The Anthropic Cosmological Principle.* Clarendon, Oxford, 1986.

[12] Mark A. Bedau. Downward causation and the autonomy of weak emergence. *Principia*, 6:5–50, 2002.

[13] Mark A. Bedau, John S. McCaskill, Norman H. Packard, Steen Rasmussen, Chris Adami, David G. Green, Takashi Ikegami, Kinihiko Kaneko, and Thomas S. Ray. Open problems in artificial life. *Artificial Life*, 6:363–376, 2000.

[14] Mark A. Bedau, Emile Snyder, and Norman H. Packard. A classification of long-term evolutionary dynamics. In Chris Adami, Richard Belew, Hiroaki Kitano, and Charles Taylor, editors, *Artificial Life VI*, pages 228–237, Cambridge, Mass., 1998. MIT Press.

[15] Michael J. Benton. Biodiversity on land and in the sea. *Geological Journal*, 36:211–230, 2001.

[16] Susan Blackmore. The grand illusion. *New Scientist*, 2348:26, 2002. 22nd June.

[17] Martin Bohner and Allan Peterson. *Dynamic Equations on Time Scales*. Birkhäuser, Boston, 2001.

[18] George Boolos. *The Logic of Provability*. Cambridge UP, Cambridge, 1993.

[19] Nick Bostrom. Causation, indexical facts &self-sampling: Exchange between Nick Bostrom and Jacques Mallah. Everything List.

[20] Nick Bostrom. *Observational Selection Effects and Probability*. PhD thesis, Dept. Philosophy, Logic and Scientific Methods London School of Economics, 2000. http://www.anthropic-principle.com/phd.

[21] Nick Bostrom. *Anthropic Bias: Observation Selection Effects in Science and Philosophy*. Routledge, New York, 2002.

[22] Nick Bostrom. Are you living in a computer simulation? *Philosophical Quarterly*, 53:243–255, 2003.

[23] Mark Buchanan. Double jeopardy. *New Scientist*, 2504:32–35, 2005.

[24] Richard W. Byrne and Andrew Whiten, editors. *Machiavellian Intelligence: Social Expertise and the Evolution of Intellect in Monkeys, Apes, and Humans.* Oxford UP, 1989.

[25] Bruce A. Carnes, D. Jay Olshansky, and Douglas Grahn. Biological evidence for limits to the duration of life. *Biogerontology*, pages 31–45, 2003.

[26] David J. Chalmers. Consciousness and its place in nature. In David J. Chalmers, editor, *Philosophy of Mind: Classical and Contemporary Readings*, chapter 27, pages 247–272. Oxford UP, Oxford, 2002. Reprinted from Blackwell Guide to the Philosophy of Mind, Stich and Warfield (eds).

[27] Richard Chang, Benny Chor, Oded Goldreich, Juris Hartmanis, Johan Håstad, Desh Ranjan, and Pankaj Rohatgi. The random oracle hypothesis is false. *Journal of Computer and System Sciences*, 49:24–39, 1994.

[28] Marcus Chown. Dying to know - would you lay your life on the line for a theory? *New Scientist*, 2113:50, 20th December 1997.

[29] Marcus Chown. Looking for alien intelligence in the computational universe. *New Scientist*, 2527:30, 26th February 2005.

[30] Daphne Chung. It's a jungle in there. *New Scientist*, 2444:42, 2004.

[31] Donald L. Cohn. *Measure Theory*. Birkhäuser, Boston, 1980.

[32] John H. Conway. What is life? In E. Berlekamp, J. H. Conway, and R. Guy, editors, *Winning Ways for your Mathematical Plays*, volume 2, chapter 25. Academic, New York, 1982.

[33] Lee Corbin. What relation do mathematical models have with reality? Everything List.

[34] John Damuth. Of size and abundance. *Nature*, 351:268–269, 1991.

[35] Paul Davies. A brief history of the Multiverse. *New York Times*, April 12 2003.

[36] Richard Dawkins. *The Selfish Gene*. Oxford UP, Oxford, 1976.

[37] Karel de Leeuw, Edward F. Moore, Claude E. Shannon, and N. Shapiro. Computation by probabilistic machines. In Shannon and McCarthy, editors, *Automata Studies*, pages 183–212. Princeton UP, Princeton, 1956.

[38] Dominique J-F de Quervain, Urs Fischbacher, Valerie Treyer, Melanie Schellhammer, et al. The neural basis of altruistic punishment. *Science*, 305:1254–1259, 2005.

[39] Bryce de Witt and R. Neill Graham. *The Many Worlds Interpretation of Quantum Mechanics*. Princeton UP, 1973.

[40] K. G. Denbigh and J. Denbigh. *Entropy in Relation to Incomplete Knowledge*. Cambridge UP, 1987.

[41] Daniel C. Dennett. *Consciousness Explained*. Allen Lane, 1991.

[42] Daniel C. Dennett. *Darwin's Dangerous Idea: Evolution and the Meaning of Life*. Simon and Schuster, 1995.

[43] David Deutsch. *The Fabric of Reality*. Penguin, 1997.

[44] David Deutsch. The structure of the Multiverse. *Proceedings of the Royal Society A*, 458:2911–2923, 2002. arXiv:quant-ph/0104033.

[45] A. Einstein, B. Podolsky, and N. Rosen. Can quantum mechanical description of physical reality be considered complete. *Phys. Rev.*, 47:777, 1935.

[46] Glenn Elert. The chaos hypertextbook. http://hypertextbook.com/chaos/.

[47] Dylan Evans. The arbitrary ape. *New Scientist*, 2148:32, 1998.

[48] Richard P. Feynman. *Surely you're Joking, Mr. Feynman! : Adventures of a Curious Character*. W.W. Norton, New York, 1985.

[49] Richard P. Feynman, Robert B. Leighton, and Matthew Sands. *The Feynman Lectures on Physics*, volume 2. Addison Wesley, 1964.

[50] Willem Fouché. Arithmetical representations of Brownian motion. *J. Symbolic Logic*, 65:421–442, 2000.

[51] Walter J. Freeman. The physiology of perception. *Scientific American*, 264:78–85, 1991.

[52] Jochen Fromm. *The Emergence of Complexity.* Kassel UP, 2004.

[53] Murray Gell-Mann. *The Quark and the Jaguar: Adventures in the Simple and the Complex.* Freeman, 1994.

[54] Jim Giles. Internet encyclopaedias go head to head. *Nature*, pages 900–901, 2005.

[55] James Gleick. *Chaos — Making a New Science.* Penguin, Harmondsworth, Middlesex, 1987.

[56] Kurt Gödel. Über formal unentscheidbare Sätze der *Principia Mathematica* und verwandter Systeme I. *Monatshefte für Mathematik und Physik*, 38:173–198, 1931.

[57] Susan Greenfield. Sensational minds. *New Scientist*, 2328:30, 2002.

[58] Felix Hausdorff. Dimension und äusseres Mass. *Math. Annalen*, 79, 1919.

[59] Stephen Hawking. *A Brief History of Time.* Bantam, New York, 1988.

[60] Jame Higgo. Does the 'many-worlds' interpretation of quantum mechanics imply immortality? http://www.higgo.com/quantum/qti.htm, 1998.

[61] James Higgo. Quantum theory of immortality. http://www.higgo.com/qti/.

[62] James Higgo. Rainer plaga's paper. Everything List.

[63] James Higgo. Quantum physics and the pensions crisis.   http://higgo.com/quantum/modest.htm, 1998.

[64] David Hilbert. Neubegründung der Mathematik: Erste Mitteilung. *Abhandlungen aus dem Seminar der Hamburgischen Universität*, 1:157–77, 1922.

[65] Douglas R. Hofstadter. *Gödel, Escher, Bach: an Eternal Golden Braid*. Harvester, 1979.

[66] Douglas R. Hofstadter. Prelude... ant fugue. In *The Mind's I : Fantasies and Reflections on Self and Soul*, page 149. Basic Books, New York, 1981.

[67] F. Hoyle, D. N.F.Dunbar, W. A. Wenzel, and W. Whaling. A state in C^{12} predicted by astrophysical evidence. *Phys. Rev.*, 92:1095, 1953.

[68] Jonathan Huebner. A possible declining trend for worldwide innovation. *Technological Forecasting and Social Change*, 72:980–986, 2005.

[69] G. E. Hutchinson and Robert J. MacArthur. A theoretical ecological model of size distributions among species of animals. *American Naturalist*, 93:117–125, 1959.

[70] J. Richard Gott III. Implications of the Copernican principle for our future prospects. *Nature*, 363:315–319, 1993.

[71] Oeppen J. and Vaupel J. W. Broken limits to life expectancy. *Science*, 296:1029–1031, 2002.

[72] Alister Kershaw. *A History of the Guillotine*. Calder, London, 1958.

[73] Raymond Kurzeil. *The Singularity Is Near: When Humans Transcend Biology.* Viking, 2005.

[74] Ray Kurzweil and Terry Grossman. *Fantastic Voyage.* Rodale, 2004. http://fantastic-voyage.net/.

[75] John Leslie. *Universes.* Routledge, New York, 1989.

[76] John Leslie. A difficulty for Everett's many-worlds theory. *International Studies in the Philosophy of Science*, 10:239–246, 1996.

[77] John Leslie. *The End of the World.* Routledge, London, 1996.

[78] John Leslie and James Higgo. Thanks for the papers etc.: Exchange between James Higgo and John Leslie regarding the possibility that qti annuls the doomsday argument. Everything List.

[79] Jeffrey Levinton. The big bang of animal evolution. *Scientific American*, 267:84–91, November 1992.

[80] Richard C. Lewontin. The units of selection. *Annual Review of Ecology and Systematics*, 1:1, 1970.

[81] Ming Li and Paul Vitányi. *An Introduction to Kolmogorov Complexity and its Applications.* Springer, New York, 2nd edition, 1997.

[82] Charles Lineweaver. An estimate of the age distribution of terrestrial planets in the universe: Quantifying metallicity as a selection effect. *Icarus*, 151:307–313, 2001. arXiv:astro-ph/0012399.

[83] Michael Lockwood. *Mind, Brain and the Quantum: The Compound 'I'.* Basil Blackwell, Oxford, 1989.

[84] Alistair Malcolm. Plausibility of the existence of all possible states. sighted at http://www.physica.freeserve.co.uk/pa01.htm.

[85] Alistair Malcolm and Russell Standish. White rabbits, measure and Max. Everything List.

[86] Jacques Mallah, Russell Standish, et al. Mallah's self sampling assumption argument. James Higgo summarised this debate at http://higgo.com/qti/Mallah.htm, and also http://www.higgo.com/quantum/qtie3.htm.

[87] Chris Maloney. Zombie wives. Everything List.

[88] Benoît Mandelbrot. *The Fractal Geometry of Nature*. W H Freeman & Co, 1982.

[89] Bruno Marchal. The origin of physical laws and sensations. Invited talk at SANE'2004, http://iridia.ulb.ac.be/~marchal.

[90] Bruno Marchal. Universal prior — go FORTH and run backward. Everything List.

[91] Bruno Marchal. Zombie wives/cul-de-sac branches. Everything List.

[92] Bruno Marchal. Informatique théorique et philosophie de l'esprit. In *Actes de 3ème colloque internatial de l'ARC*, pages 193–227, Toulouse, 1988.

[93] Bruno Marchal. Mechanism and personal identity. In M. de Glas and D. Gabbay, editors, *Proceedings of WOCFAI '91*, pages 335–345, Paris, 1991. Angkor.

[94] Bruno Marchal. *Calculabilité, Physique et Cognition.* PhD thesis, Université de Lille, 1998. http://iridia.ulb.ac.be/~marchal/.

[95] Bruno Marchal. Computation, consciousness and the quantum. *Teorie e modelli*, 6(1):29–44, 2001.

[96] Tim Maudlin. Computation and consciousness. *J. Philosophy*, 86:407–432, 1989.

[97] Simon McGregor and Chrisantha Fernando. Levels of description; a novel approach to dynamical hierarchies. *Artificial Life*, 11:459–472, 2005.

[98] Daniel W. McShea. Metazoan complexity and evolution: Is there a trend? *Evolution*, 50:477–492, 1996.

[99] John McTaggart. The unreality of time. *Mind: A Quarterly Review of Psychology and Philosophy*, 17:456–473, 1908.

[100] Steven Mithen. *The Prehistory of the Mind.* Thames and Hudson, 1996.

[101] Hans Morovic. *Mind Children.* Harvard UP, 1989.

[102] Toby Ord. Hypercomputation: computing more than a Turing machine. Technical report, Dept. Philosophy, Univ. Melbourne, 2002. arXiv:math.LO/0209332.

[103] Don N. Page. Observational consequences of many-worlds quantum theory. Technical Report Alberta-Thy-04-99, Institute for Theoretical Physics, U. Alberta, 1999. arXiv:quant-th/9904004.

[104] Stephanie Pain. Mud, glorious mud — to human eyes the deep sea looks a singularly unpromising place for life to flourish. to the millions of tiny creatures that live there, it's every bit as rich as a tropical rainforest. *New Scientist*, 2054, 2 November 1996.

[105] Roger Penrose. *The Emperor's New Mind: Concerning Computers, Minds, and the Laws of Physics.* Oxford UP, Oxford, 1989.

[106] Petrus Potgieter. Zeno machines and hypercomputation. arXiv:cs.CC/0412022.

[107] Michael Clive Price. Many worlds FAQ. http://www.hedweb.com/manworld.htm.

[108] Jr. R. S. van Dyck, P. B. Schwinberg, and H. G. Dehmelt. Precise measurements of axial, magnetron, cyclotron, and spin-cyclotron-beat frequencies on an isolated 1-MeV electron. *Phys. Rev. Lett.*, 38:310, 1977.

[109] Tom Ray. An approach to the synthesis of life. In C. G. Langton, C. Taylor, J. D. Farmer, and S. Rasmussen, editors, *Artificial Life II*, page 371. Addison-Wesley, Reading, Mass., 1991.

[110] Hal Ruhl. My proposed model - short form. Everything List.

[111] Jürgen Schmidhuber. A computer scientist's view of life, the universe and everything. In C. Freska, M. Jantzen, and R. Valk, editors, *Foundations of Computer Science: Potential-Theory-Cognition*, volume 1337 of *Lecture Notes in Computer Science*, pages 201–208. Springer, Berlin, 1997.

[112] Jürgen Schmidhuber. Algorithmic theories of everything. Technical Report IDSIA-20-00, IDSIA, Galleria 2, 6928 Manno (Lugano), Switzerland, 2000. arXiv:quant-ph/0011122.

[113] Jean Schneider. Extra-solar planets catalog. http://www.obspm.fr/encycl/catalog.html.

[114] Erwin Schrödinger. Die gegenwärtige Situation in der Quantenmechanik. *Naturwissenschaften*, 48:807, 1935.

[115] Sanjeev S. Seahra and Paul S. Wesson. The universe as a five-dimensional black hole. *General Relativity and Gravitation*, 37:1339–1347, 2005.

[116] André Seznec and Nicolas Sendrier. HAVEGE: A user-level software heuristic for generating empirically strong random numbers. *ACM Transactions on Modeling and Computer Simulation*, 13:334–346, 2003.

[117] Ramamurti Shankar. *Principles of Quantum Mechanics*. Plenum, New York, 1980.

[118] Evan Siemann, David Tilman, and John Haarstad. Abundance, diversity and body size: Patterns from a grassland arthropod community. *Journal of Animal Ecology*, 68:824–835, 1999.

[119] André Skusa and Mark Bedau. Towards a comparison of evolutionary creativity in biological and cultural evolution. In Russell Standish, Hussein Abbass, and Mark Bedau, editors, *Artificial Life VIII*, page 233. MIT Press, Cambridge, Mass., 2002. online at http://alife8.alife.org.

[120] John Maynard Smith and Eörs Szathmáry. *The Major Transitions in Evolution.* Oxford UP, 1995.

[121] Lee Smolin. *The Life of the Cosmos.* Oxford University Press, 1997.

[122] Lee Smolin. *Three Roads to Quantum Gravity.* Basic Books, New York, 2001.

[123] Euan Squires. *The Mystery of the Quantum World.* Institute of Physics, 1986.

[124] Russell K. Standish. Evolution in the Multiverse. *Complexity International*, 7, 2000. arXiv:physics/0001021.

[125] Russell K. Standish. On complexity and emergence. *Complexity International*, 9, 2001. arXiv:nlin.AO/0101006.

[126] Russell K. Standish. Open-ended artificial evolution. *International Journal of Computational Intelligence and Applications*, 3:167, 2003. arXiv:nlin.AO/0210027.

[127] Russell K. Standish. The influence of parsimony and randomness on complexity growth in Tierra. In Bedau et al., editors, *ALife IX Workshop and Tutorial Proceedings*, pages 51–55, 2004. arXiv:nlin.AO/0604026.

[128] Russell K. Standish. Why Occam's razor? *Foundations of Physics Letters*, 17:255–266, 2004. arXiv:physics/0001020.

[129] Henry P. Stapp. *Mind, Matter and Quantum Mechanics.* Springer, Berlin, 1993.

[130] Victor Stenger. *Where Do The Laws Of Physics Come From?: The Comprehensible Cosmos.* Prometheus, Amherst, NY, 2006.

[131] Ian Stewart. *Does God Play Dice? The Mathematics of Chaos.* Penguin, Harmondsworth, Middlesex, 1989.

[132] Ian Stewart and Jack Cohen. *Figments of Reality.* Cambridge UP, 1997.

[133] Max Tegmark. Amoeba croaks. Everything List.

[134] Max Tegmark. Is "the Theory of Everything" merely the ultimate ensemble theory. *Annals of Physics*, 270:1–51, 1998.

[135] Max Tegmark. The importance of quantum decoherence in brain processes. *Phys. Rev. E*, 61:4194–4206, 2000. arXiv:quant-ph/9907009.

[136] Max Tegmark. Parallel universes. In J. D. Barrow, P. C. W. Davies, and Jr. C. L. Harper, editors, *Science and Ultimate Reality: From Quantum to Cosmos*, chapter 21, pages 459–491. Cambridge UP, Cambridge, 2003. arXiv:astro-ph/0302131.

[137] Frank J. Tipler. *The Physics of Immortality.* Doubleday, 1994.

[138] Alan Turing. Computing machinery and intelligence. *Mind*, 59:433–460, 1950. sighted at http://www.loebner.net/Prizef/TuringArticle.html.

[139] United Nations Population Division. *The World at Six Billion.* http://www.un.org/esa/population/publications/sixbillion/sixbillion.htm.

[140] United Nations Population Division. *World Population Prospects: The 2004 Revision*, 2005. http://www.unpopulation.org.

[141] US Census Bureau. *Historical Estimates of World Population*. http://www.census.gov/ipc/www/worldhis.html.

[142] US Census Bureau. *IDB — Rank Countries by Population*. http://www.census.gov/ipc/www/idbrank.html.

[143] Vernor Vinge. The coming technological singularity. http://en.wikisource.org/wiki/ The_Coming_Technological_Singularity.

[144] Duncan Watts. *Six Degrees : the Science of a Connected Age*. Norton, New York, 2003.

[145] Daniel Wegner. *The Illusion of Conscious Will*. MIT Press, Cambridge, MA, 2002.

[146] Steven Weinberg. *Dreams of a Final Theory*. Pantheon, New York, 1992.

[147] Alex A. S. Weir, Jackie Chappell, and Alex Kacelnik. Shaping of hooks in New Caledonian crows. *Science*, 297:981, 2002.

[148] Peter Weiss. Dr. feynman's doodles. *Science News*, 168:40, 2005. http://www.sciencenews.org/articles/20050716/bob9.asp.

[149] Paul S. Wesson. Enter the void. *New Scientist*, 2538:32–35, 11th Feb 2006.

[150] John A. Wheeler. Time today. In J.J. Halliwell, J. Perez-Mercador, and W.H.Zurek, editors, *Physical Origins of Time Assymetry*, pages 1–29. Cambridge UP, 1994.

[151] Andrew Whiten and Richard W. Byrne, editors. *Machiavellian Intelligence II: Extensions and Evaluations*. Oxford UP, 1997.

[152] E. P. Wigner. *Symmetries and Reflections*. MIT Press, Cambridge, 1967.

[153] Stephen Wolfram. *A New Kind of Science*. Wolfram Media, 2002. online at http://www.wolframscience.com.

[154] Eliezer S. Yudkowsky. Staring into the singularity. sighted at http://sysopmind.com/singularity.html.

[155] Konrad Zuse. *Rechender Raum, Schriften zur Datenverarbeitung Band 1*. Friedrich Vieweg & Sohn, Braunschweig, 1969.

Index

Δ (difference), 204

$\aleph_0$, 201

$\cap$ (intersection), 199

$\cup$ (union), 199

$\emptyset$, *see* empty set

$\int$ (integral), 204

∇ (vector derivative), 206

$\sum$ (sum), 203

3-body problem, 27

Adam paradox, 88

Adami, Chris, 108

Adams, Douglas, 70, 97, 155

adaption, 109

adjoint, 197

aeroplane crash, 138

AI thesis, 71

AIT, *see* algorithmic information theory

aleph null, *see* $\aleph_0$

algorithmic information theory, 5, 7, *32*, 46

Alice in Wonderland, 59

altruism, 151, 173, 184

Amari, Shun-ichi, 135

American sign language, 95

ANN, *see* artificial neural network

ant, 90

    nest, 94

anthropic

    principle, 9, 16, 56, 79, *81–84*, 89, 112, 162, 164, 166, 178, 181

    reasoning, 17, 94

    selection, 18, 28, *89*, 101, 102, 113, 119, 213, 217

artificial intelligence, 71, 103, 106

artificial life, 108

artificial neural networks, 104

Aspect, Alain, 54

ASSA, *see* self sampling assumption, absolute

attractor, 105

Augustine, Saint, 151

autostimulation, 171
Avida, 108
axiom, 15, 162

Banach space, 68
baptism, 151
Barrow, John, 43, 83
beauty, 58
Bedau, Mark, 26, 109
beetles, 93
beginning, 21
Bell's theorem, 155
Benton, Michael, 102
beta decay, 112
bird perspective, 74, 101,
        159
Bishop Berkley, 164
black hole, 48, 49
block Multiverse, 162
Bohm pilot wave theory,
        54
Bohm, David, 175
Bohr, Nils, 175
Boltzmann-Gibbs, 35
Bonaparte, Napoleon, 165
bonobos, 94
bootstrap, 164
Borges, Jorge, 14, 34
Born rule, *117*, 118, 130,
        147, 220
Bostrom, Nick, 66, 85, 89
broken stick model, 90
Brownian motion, 73, 97
butterfly effect, 13, 17, 24,
        106

calculus
        differential, 205
        integral, 205
Cambrian explosion, 109
Cantor set, 65
Cantor, Georg, 201
cardinality, 199
Carrol, Lewis, 59
Carter, Brandon, 85
Cartesian unity, 78
Category theory, 46
causality, 18
        downward, 27, 162
        reverse, 149
cellular automaton, 60
centrifugal force, 156
centripetal force, 156
Chaitin, Greg, 37
Chalmers, David, 176, 185
chaos, 24, 105, 171
chimpanzee, 94
Chinese argument, 90
Chinese Room argument,
        168
Church-Turing thesis, 73
clock, 67, 221
Cogito ergo sum, 83, 159
COMP, *125–129*
complement, 199
complex conjugate, 196,
        197
complex measure, 68
complex number, *see* num-
        ber, complex

complexity, 5, 12, 15, 21, 31, 34, 39, *39–40*, 43, 45, 58, 62, 108, 110, 145
computational irreducibility, 27
computationalism, 16, 17, 70, 71, *71–79*, 125, 129, 130, 143, 153, 165
conic section, 27
consciousness, 13, 17, 18, 22, 28, 72, 77, 79, 84, 88, 90, 94, 103, 125, 139, 143, 144, *155–180*, 182, 185
consistent histories, 176
contingency, 56, 89
continuum hypothesis, 202
Copenhagen Interpretation, 4, 7, 54, 175
correspondence principle, 117, 120, 130
counterfactuals, 75
Cramer-Rao, 124
creationism, 100
creativity, 17, 18, 72, *102–113*, 168
Crichton, Kim, 242
Crichton-Standish, Hal, 242
cryptic program, *111*
cul-de-sac, *139–140*, 142, 143, 149
cultural evolution, 99

Damuth's law, 93
Darwin, Charles, 97
Davies, Paul, 51
Dawkins, Richard, 98
de Quervain, Dominique, 151
de Witt, Bryce, 47
decapitation, 140
dementia, 143, 185
Dennett, Daniel, 83, 97, 170
Dent, Arthur, 70
derivative, 205
    partial, 205
Descartes, René, 83, 159, 170, 177
description, 5, *32*, 39, *45*, 60, 62, 67, 79
determinism, 184
Deutsch, David, 4, 7, 11, 18, 55, 77, 83, 115, 144, 162
diagonalisation, 201
differentiation, 144
Ding an sich, 159
diversity, 102, 109
dog, 95, 172
dolphin, 94, 172
Doomsday Argument, 17, *84–89*, 145
downward causation, 177
dragons, 62
dual, 45, 67, 119
dualism, 177

dynamical systems, 26, 105

eigenvalue, 4, 117, 123, *197–199*
Einstein, Albert, 3, 58, 100
elephant, 179
eliminative materialism, 177
emergence, 8, 12, 21, *22–28*, 110, 158, 162, 178
  nominal, 26
  strong, 27, 162
  weak, 27
empty set, 199
endosymbiosis, 110
ensemble, 7, 11, 13, *43–55*
entropy, 25, *34–37*, 157
epiphenomenon, 162
epiphenomenonalism, 178
EPR experiment, 3
equivalence class, 32
ergodic, 35
Euclid's fifth axiom, 131
Euclidean, 122, 131
eukaryote, 110
euthanasia, 150
event horizon, 48
Everything, 5, 15, 40, 43, *45*, 61
Everything list, *8*, 18, 66, 68, 125, 138, 150, 166

evolution, 7, 17, 18, 49, 61, *98–113*, 118, 134, 164, 170, 217
evolutionary algorithm, 107
evolutionary transitions, 110
existence, 22
exponent, 188
exponential function, 189
extra-solar planets, 82
Extreme Physical Information, 123–125

Fabric of Reality list, 167
falsification, 7, 9, 99, 107, 181
Fehr, Ernst, 151
Feynman, Richard, 43, 54, 115
field, 194
filmed graph, 75, 76
fine structure constant, 81
fine tuning, 16
finite axiomatic systems, 52
Finney, Hal, 147
first cause, 163
first person, 74, 159
Fisher information, 123, 135
fractal, 65, 203
free will, 18, 22, 28, 152, 155, *166–169*, 173, 184
Freeman, Walter, 106

Frieden, Roy, 123, 135
frog perspective, 74, 101, 159
functionalism, 13, *69–71*, 144, 185

Gödel, Kurt, 52
Gallup, Gordon, 94
Game of Life, 134
gauge invariance, 121, 130
Gauss, Carl Friedrich, 192
gcc, 165
Gell-Mann, Murray, 34, 54
geodesic, 157
Gilman, Charlotte, 137
God, 21, 42, 55, 82, 93, 100, 165, 174, 182, 183
golden rule, 152
gorilla, 94
Gott III, Richard, 85
grandfather paradox, 149
gravitation, 10, 100, 105
gravity, 157
Great Computer, 61
Great Programmer, 184
group, 193
Grover's algorithm, 113
guillotine, 140

Haldane, J.B.S., 93
Halting problem, 53, 201
hard problem, 177, 185
Harry Potter world, 59

Hausdorff dimension, 65
HAVEGE, 72
Hawking, Stephen, 5, 9, 54, 79, 165, 187
heaven, 151, 184
Heisenberg uncertainty principle, 30
Heisenberg, Werner, 175
hell, 151, 184
heritability, 101, 119
Hermitian, 116, 117, 197, 222
Higgo, James, 138, 150
Hilbert programme, 52
Hilbert space, 117, 129, 221
history, 67
Hitchhiker's Guide to the Galaxy, 70, 97
HLUT, *see* huge lookup table
Hofstadter, Douglas, 94
Hoyle, Fred, 82
Huebner, Jonathon, 103
huge lookup table, 168
Huxley, Thomas, 163
hypercomputation, 73
hypothesis, 165, 181

I think, therefore I am, 83
ideal gas, 35
idealism, 159
illusion, *155–161*, 161, 168
imaginary

number, 161
time, 187
immortality, 69, 137
inertial reference frame, 156
infinite regression, 163
inflation, 48, 53
information, 5, 12, 15, *31*, 34, 39
information theory, *see* algorithmic information theory
inner product, 196
instrumentalism, 116
integer, 190, 194
integration, 204
irreversibility, 22, 26

justice, 152

Kant, Immanuel, 159
KCS complexity, *39*
Kelvin, Lord, 98
King Midas, 149
Klara, 75, 144, 167
knowledge, 127
Koko, 94
Kolmogorov probability axioms, 217
Kolmogorov, Andrey, 37
Koza, John, 107
Kripke semantics, 142
Kuhn, Thomas, 7

Löbian machine, 160

language, 23, 99, 108, 163
incommensurate, 25
semantic, 23, 25
syntactic, 23
Languille, 141
Laplace's daemon, 37, 157
Laplace, Pierre-Simon, 165
Lavoisier, Antoine, 140
legal entitity, 173
legal responsibility, 173
Leslie, John, 85, 145
Lewontin, Richard, 101, 102, 118, 221
Library of Babel, 14, 34, 43, 60
life, 22, 170
linear operator, 197
linearity, 119, 130, *196*
Lineweaver, Charlie, 82
Lockwood, Michael, 77, 177
logarithm, 188
Lorenz, Edward, 24
Lorenz, Konrad, 181
lottery, 147

Müller-Lyer illusion, 158
Machiavellian Intelligence, 171
macroscopic, 25, 35
Malcolm, Alistair, 61
Mallah, Jacques, 145–147
Many Worlds Interpretation, 4, 6, 7, 30,

47, 54, 67, 138, 175, 176
map, 189
   territory, 5, 79
Marchal, Bruno, 50, 69, 74, 125, 147, 160, 165, 201
Margulis, Lynn, 110
materialism, 159, 177
mathematics, 15
matrix, 197
Matrix (the movie), 83
Maudlin, Tim, 75, 144, 167
Maynard Smith, John, 110
meaning, 13, 15, 32
measure, *67–69*, 118, 203, 219
   complex, 219
   spectral, 215
   uniform, 145
   zero, 65, 203
meme, 98
microscopic, 25, 35
mimetics, 99
mind-body problem, 162
Minkowski spacetime, 121, 131, 161
miracle, 62, 184
mirror test, 94
Mithen, Steven, 172
Mitra, Saibal, 147
modal logic, 125–128
monism, 178

Moore's law, 152
moral responsibility, 174
Morovic transfer, 87
Multiverse, 13, 28, 30, 42, *47*, 49, 53, 73, 74, 77, 88, 101, 102, 112, 120, 142, 144, 147, 149, 159, 160, 167, 175, 176, 183, 186
MWI, *see* Many Worlds Interpretation

Nürnberg trials, 174
natural selection, 98, 101, 102
necessity, 56, 89
New Caledonian crow, 168
Newton's first law, 156
Newton, Isaac, 100
no cul-de-sac conjecture, 142, 143, 147
Nothing, 5, 15, 21, 40, 43, *45*, 51, 160
noumenon, 159
NP hard, 112
number
   complex, 118, 192, 194, 219
   irrational, 190
   natural, 189
   rational, 189, 194
   real, 194
   whole, 189, 194

objective, 74
objectivity, 28
observable, 117
observer, 8, 18, *28*, 31, 32, 34, 39, 49, 55, 61, 64, 79, 81, 83, 85, 101, 119
observer moment, 59, *66–67*, 118, 142, 145, 161, 175, 217
Occam
    catastrophe, 83, 164
    razor, 11, 15, 40, 42, *57–58*, 60, 83, 121, 132, 163, 181
        theorem, 58, 89
octonian, 193
old age, 139
Olympia, 75, 144, 167
open-ended evolution, 108
orangutan, 94

$P \neq NP$, 111
Packard, Norm, 109
Page, Don, 138
Papaioannou, Stathis, 147
Pareto front, 29
participatory universe, 81
path integral formulation, 115
Penrose, Roger, 77
pension, 149
phenomenon, 159
physicalism, 59, 70, 177
Planck scale, 64

Plato, 14, 49, 55, 76, 128, 176
    aviary, 170
Platonism, 49
Plenitude, *49*, 51, 52, 55, 60, 62, 79, 130, 144, 160, 165, 176, 178
Popper, Karl, 7, 9, 99, 181
post-modernism, 30
posthuman, 87
predator confusion, 169
prime mover, 184
probability, 68
problem of induction, 59
PROJECTION postulate, *119*, 129, 182, 217
prokaryote, 110
pseudo force, 156
punishment, 173
Pythagoras's theorem, 121, 131

QTI, *see* quantum, immortality
qualia, 160
quantum
    chromodynamics, 28
    computer, 77, 112
    gravity, 10, 11, 28
        loop, 10
    immortality, 6, 13, 18, 88, *138–153*, 184
    logic, 128

mechanics, 2, 4, 8, 10,
    13, 17, 30, 47, 49,
    54, 73, 77, 102,
    113, 115, *115–136*,
    149, 161, 175, 182,
    185
  roulette, 6
  state, 4
  suicide, 148, 149
quark, 28
quaternion, 193

radioactivity, 98
/dev/random, 72
randomness, 17, *32*, 50,
    61, 71, 72, 78, 97,
    112, 168
rational numbers, 65
Ray, Tom, 108
realism, 176
reality, 156
reductionism, 23, 25
reincarnation, 143, 185
relativity, 30, 131
  general, 10, 48, 64,
    100, 157, 182
  special, 4, 121
religion, 152
reversibility, 22, 26
Romeo and Juliet, 32, 34
Rorshach test, 62
RSA algorithm, 111
RSSA, *see* self sampling
    assumption, rel-
    ative

Ruhl, Hal, 45
Russell, Bertrand, 163

Schmidhuber, Jürgen, 49,
    52, 61, 71
Schrödinger
  cat, 2, 5, 137
  equation, 4, 74, 101,
    102, *116*, 130, 222
scientific, 99
Searle, John, 168
second law of thermody-
    namics, *25*, 34, 101,
    157
selection, 101, 102
  anthropic, *see* anthropic,
    selection
  natural, *see* natural
    selection
self sampling assumption,
    85, 118, 137
  absolute, *147*
  relative, *147*
  strong, 66, 145, *146*
self-awareness, 17, 18, *84*,
    94, *163*, 169, 182,
    186
semantic language, 28, 158
set, 199
Shakespeare, William, 32
shut up and calculate, 116,
    118
simplicity, 58
singularity, technological,
    87, 153

six degrees of separation, 151

small world, 151, 184

Smolin, Lee, 10, 49, 102

solipsism, 164, 183

Solomonoff, Ray, 37, 58

Solomonoff-Levi distribution, 58

Something, 5

soul, 69, 107

spectral measure, 68

speed prior, 61

Squires, Euan, 138

SSA, *see* self sampling assumption

standard model, 10

Standish, Russell, 8, 26, 32, 61, 64, 89, 109, 112, 118, 147

Stapp, Henry, 78

Stenger, Victor, 121

strange loop, 162

string theory, 10, 28, 64

subjective, 74

superannuation, 149

supervenience, *69*, 78, 83, 144, 162, 178

Swift, Jonathon, 150

symmetry breaking, 55, 89

syntactic language, 28, 158

Szathmáry, Eörs, 110

technology, 99

Tegmark, Max, 6, 7, 11, 14, 44, 48, 52, 78, 131, 133, 137, 159

Teller, Edward, 138

Theaetetus, 128

theology, 183

theorem, 15

Theory of Everything, 7, 10, 13

Theory of Nothing, 9

theory of the mind, 171

thermodynamic, 37

third person, 74, 159

three body problem, *see* 3-body problem

Tierra, 108, 112

time, *63–65*, 155, 161–162, 185

    proper, 64

    psychological, 64, 161

    scale, 65

TIME postulate, 16, *64*, 66, 129, 143, 146, 161, 182

Turing machine, 39, 51, 58, 71–73, 111, 165

Turing test, 75

Turing, Alan, 103, 201

turtles all the way down, 163

uncomputable numbers, 53

unitarity, 4, 130, 146

unitary, 198

universal dovetailer, 50,
        61, 128
Universal Dovetailer Ar-
        gument, 51, 78
universal prior, 58
universe, 67

vacuum, 43
variation, 101, 102
vector, *194–199*
vector space, 117
virtual reality, 16, 83
vitalism, 107, 170
von Neumann, John, 175

warranty period, 139
wavefunction, 118, 175
wavefunction collapse, 4,
        175
Wheeler, John, 47, 81
White Rabbit problem, *59–
        63*, 105, 182
Wigner, E.P., 13
Wikipedia, 188
Wolfram, Stephen, 60
Word, 21
world, 67

Yes Doctor, 70, 74

zero information, 15
zero information princi-
        ple, 55
Zipf's law, 90
zombies, 166
Zuse, Konrad, 60